D1478095

Microsoft® Office 2004
Step by Step

Macintosh Edition

Word Processing with Word

Graphics with PowerPoint

Presentations with PowerPoint

Spreadsheets with Excel

Personal Data with Entourage

Computer
Literacy
Press

Cincinnati, Ohio

Bonita Sebastian • Arthur Luehrmann • Herbert Peckham

Design / InfoTech / Paul Quin
Cover / Carolyn Ayres
Production coordination / Zipporah Collins
Copyediting / Zipporah Collins
Technical checking / Zipporah Collins
Page layout / Computer Literacy Press, LLC
Imagesetting / Data Reproductions Corporation
Printing and binding / Data Reproductions Corporation

ISBN 1-57426-163-0

This entire book has been user tested on computers with Microsoft
Office 2004 and Macintosh OS 10.3. All figures in the book were created
from that software. Users of other software versions may expect to
encounter differences.

This book is a guide to learning and using Microsoft Office 2004 Macintosh
Edition, not a formal specification of the software as delivered to the buyer
now or in future software revisions. Microsoft Corporation makes no
warranties with respect to this book or to its accuracy in describing any
current or future version of Microsoft Office.

Computer Literacy Press
15 Triangle Park
Cincinnati, OH 45246

(800) 833-5413

http://www.compLitpress.com

Printed in the United States of America
10 9 8 7 6 5 4 3 2 1   01098765

Contents

Preface

Microsoft Office 2004 Step by Step is based on an old Chinese proverb: "I hear, and I forget. I see, and I remember. I do, and I understand." Each page of the book is a simple list of steps for you to do at the computer. With just a little reading and a whole lot of doing, you'll quickly see how to use each of the many Office 2004 tools for writing, editing, checking spelling, formatting text, printing form letters, using graphics tools to create appealing presentations, doing complex calculations, creating charts, working with collections of personal data, managing a project, and using e-mail.

You need not go through the whole book from beginning to end. Everyone should do pages 1–25. After that, either continue in order or jump to topics you're especially interested in. To help you navigate from topic to topic, icons in the upper-left corner of some pages warn you when some previous topic or activity should have been done first. Here's a list of icons and what they mean:

 Be sure you have completed the previous topic before beginning this one.

 Before beginning this page, be sure you previously created and saved the named document.

 Read important information here before doing the first step on this page.

A word of advice. Read each step carefully, do exactly what it says, watch the screen to see what happens, and go on to the next step. Sometimes you'll be tempted to go off and check out a few ideas on your own. *Don't give in to the temptation!* The result can change things in ways that make later steps in the book produce surprising results.

This is not to say that exploring on your own is bad. Just the reverse—you should feel free to try anything out. Just make sure you complete a set of topics in the book, save your document if necessary, and then do all the exploration you want. When you finish, discard the document you used for experimentation.

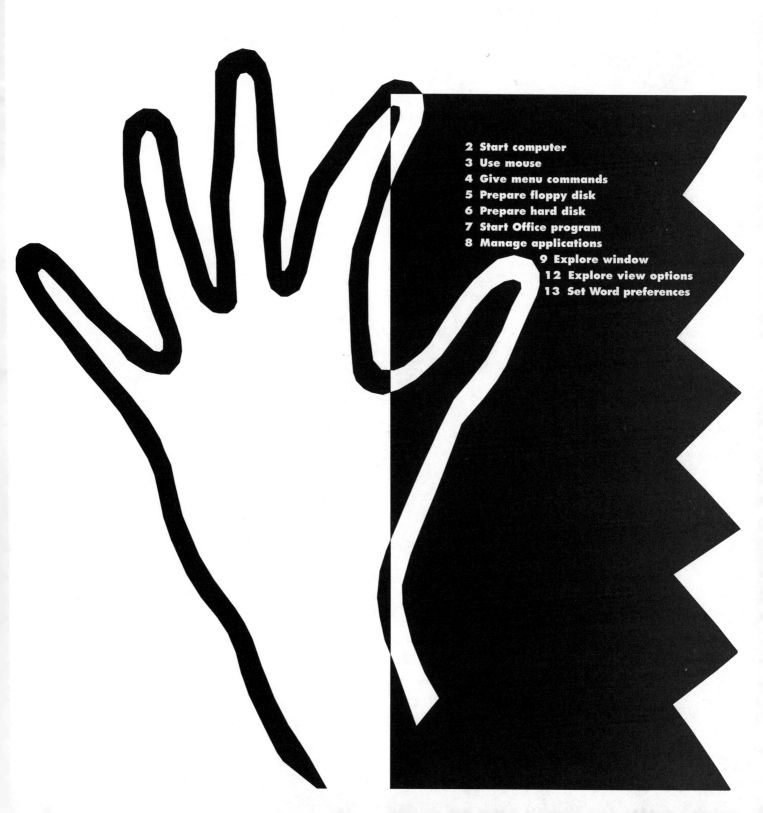

Start computer

Every session begins with starting the computer, which launches the Macintosh system software.

1 Start system software

Locate start key at top of keyboard or start button on computer.

> *Start key or button has circle broken by vertical line or has small triangle. Start button may be at front, back, or side of computer.*

Tap start key, or press and hold button. If necessary, switch on monitor.

> *It takes some minutes for system software to start up and log-in screen to appear.*

2 Log in

Click your user name; enter your password.

Click **Log in**.

3 View startup screen

> *Screen should have all features in figure. You may see others.*

Menu bar —
Desktop —
Hard disk icon—
Pointer —
Dock —

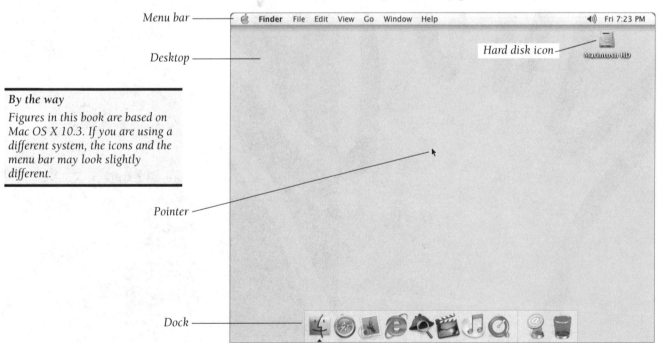

> *Small figure at upper right is called "icon." At left on menu bar, name shows that Finder application program is now running. Finder automatically starts when you start computer.*

Notice small black arrow pointer.

> *You use mouse to control pointer.*

4 View dock

> *Dock should have most icons in figure above. You may see more or fewer.*

Complete previous activity before going on.

Use mouse

To use the Macintosh, you need to use the mouse. Don't worry about getting it right the first time. You'll get lots of practice.

1 Move pointer

Hold mouse on smooth surface, wire away from you.

Watch pointer on screen as you slide mouse toward and away from you.

Watch pointer as you move mouse left and right. Move mouse in circle. Try moving pointer off screen.

2 Click object (to select it)

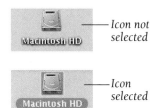
— Icon not selected
— Icon selected

Move pointer tip inside hard disk icon at upper right.

Watch hard disk icon as you tap mouse button.

Outline and shaded area surround selected icon and name.

Click in clear area of window to deselect icon.

3 Drag object (to move it)

Move pointer to hard disk icon.

With mouse button held down, move mouse left. Release mouse button.

Icon moves to pointer position and stays there.

Drag hard disk icon back to original location.

4 Double-click object (for special action)

By the way

Double-clicking means different things in different situations. When you work with text, for example, you'll see that double-clicking a word usually selects all the letters in the word.

With pointer tip inside hard disk icon, quickly tap mouse button twice.

Tapping mouse button quickly twice is called "double-clicking." Double-clicking icon is shortcut for opening it. Hard disk window appears.

5 Click button (for different action)

At upper left corner of window, notice three round buttons. Put pointer on any button. Click red button at left (close).

Window closes with single click. You'll learn more about these buttons on page 9.

Close any other windows that are open.

6 View dock

Use pointer to explore contents of dock. Notice name that appears when pointer is over item.

Small triangle under icon means item is now running on computer.

7 Open Trash from dock

Notice **Trash** icon at right end of dock. Click icon *once.*

Trash opens in separate window. Items in dock open with one click.

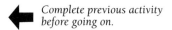

*Selected
command*

Give menu commands

*Macintosh applications always have a menu bar at the top of
the screen. You do things by choosing commands on menus.*

1 *Give menu command to close window*

Click **File** in menu bar at top of screen.

Move pointer down to **Close Window** to highlight command name.

Click highlighted command.

> Trash *window disappears. From now on in this book, steps like this are
> abbreviated as follows: "On* File *menu, choose* Close Window.*"*

2 *Give command to create new (empty) folder*

On **File** menu, choose **New Folder**.

Notice highlighted and outlined icon on desktop.

> *Outline around label means your typing will replace label.*

Type `Just a Test` as name of folder. Tap (RETURN).

> (RETURN) *is at right of main group of keys.*

3 *Give command to put new folder in Trash*

Make sure new folder icon is highlighted.

On File menu, choose **Move To Trash**.

> *Folder icon disappears.*

4 *View item in Trash*

> Trash *icon shows something inside.*

Click **Trash** icon.

> Trash *window opens. Your* Just a Test *folder is now in* Trash *window.*

5 *Give command to empty Trash*

On **Finder** menu, choose **Empty Trash**.

> *Three dots after command name mean dialog box will appear.*

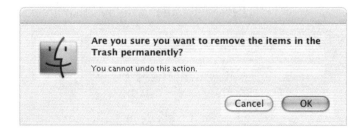

In dialog box, click **OK**.

> Trash *window closes automatically. Contents are permanently erased.*

6 *Open Trash window, then close it*

> *As you might expect,* Trash *window is empty.*

By the way

*Each application you run has its
own menus. The menus you see now
belong to the Finder. When you
start a Microsoft Office application
running, you'll see new and
changed menus.*

← *Complete previous activity before going on.*

Prepare floppy disk

If your computer has a floppy drive, you can save your work in this book on a floppy disk. If not, skip to the next page.

— *Selected for editing*

— *New disk name*

By the way

The advantage of using a floppy disk or "thumb drive" (see Tip below) is that you can take your files from one computer to another and continue working on them.

---

1 Insert formatted blank or recycled floppy disk into drive

2 Rename disk

When floppy disk icon appears on desktop, click name below icon.

Type My Disk as new floppy disk name. Tap [RETURN].

3 Erase contents, if any

Double-click floppy disk icon to see contents. If empty, skip to step 4.

On **Edit** menu, choose **Select All**.

On **File** menu, choose **Move To Trash**.

On **Finder** menu, choose **Empty Trash**. Click **OK** to approve deletion of files.

4 Create folder where work will be saved

On **View** menu, choose **as List**.

On **File** menu, choose **New Folder**.

> *Folder named* untitled folder *appears in window. Outline and highlighting mean your typing will replace name.*

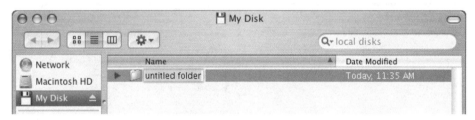

Type My Files- plus your initials as folder name. Tap [RETURN].

Close **My Disk** window.

5 Eject disk

Make sure **My Disk** icon is highlighted on desktop.

On **File** menu, choose **Eject My Disk**.

> *Step is important! Manually removing disk will leave it incomplete.*

Wait for drive activity to stop and disk to be ejected.

> *If disk isn't automatically ejected, you must press button on drive.*

Write your name on label on disk, and keep it safe.

Skip to page 7.

Tip

You can also use a "thumb drive" (a flash memory chip with a USB connector) in much the same way as a floppy disk. When you plug it in, it appears as a drive on the desktop. Do steps 2–5 to prepare it for use in this book. Then unplug it, and have it handy whenever you need to save or open files.

Prepare hard disk

If your computer has no floppy (or "thumb") drive, you'll save your files in the Documents *folder on a hard disk.*

1 **View Documents folder contents**

Make sure you are logged into user account you'll use in rest of book.

On **File** menu, choose **New Finder Window**.

In left pane of window, click **Documents**.

> Documents *folder is normally on hard disk of computer you're using. For networked computers, however, folder may be on hard disk serving other computers on network.*

On **View** menu, choose **as List**.

> *Contents of your* Documents *folder appears in right pane. Each user account has separate* Documents *folder. If you or another user has logged into this account and saved files or folders, you'll see them also listed here.*

2 **Create folder where work will be saved**

On **File** menu, choose **New Folder**.

> *Folder named* untitled folder *appears in window. Outline and highlighting mean your typing will replace name.*

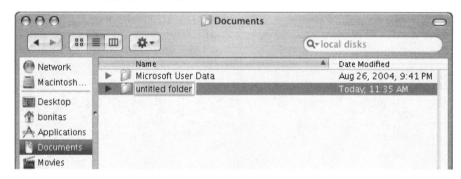

Type `My Files-` plus your initials as folder name.

Tap `RETURN`.

3 **Close Documents window**

Start Office program

The first step in using Microsoft Office is to start one of its application programs running. You'll start Microsoft Word.

1 Try opening Word from dock

If dock contains icon like one on left, click it. Skip to step 6.

2 Try using shortcut to start Microsoft Word

At far left of menu bar, click Apple icon. On pop-up menu, move pointer to **Recent Items**.

Submenu shows applications and documents recently used on computer.

If submenu contains **Microsoft Word**, click it. Skip to step 6.

3 Locate folder containing Microsoft Office application

On desktop, double-click hard disk icon to open window.

In left pane, click **Applications**.

If necessary, on **View** menu, choose **as List**.

If list is not alphabetized, click **Name** heading above list.

4 Open Microsoft Office 2004 folder

Double-click **Microsoft Office 2004** folder.

Folder ⟶

5 Start Microsoft Office application running in computer

If necessary, on **View** menu, choose **as List**. In list of items, locate application program you want (**Microsoft Word** for now).

Microsoft Office applications ⟶

Double-click **Microsoft Word** to start application running.

Microsoft Word window and menus soon appear.

6 Close Project Gallery startup window and Office Assistant

If **Project Gallery** window appears, click **Cancel**.

If Office Assistant (tiny computer on legs) appears, click tiny close button on upper left to put away.

7 If necessary, add Word shortcut to dock

Notice Word icon in dock.

Hold down (CONTROL), and click icon.

On pop-up menu, click **Keep In Dock**.

In future, shortcut in step 1 can be used to open Word.

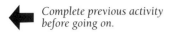 *Complete previous activity before going on.*

Manage applications

With multiple applications running at the same time, switching between them by accident is common. Here's the remedy.

1 Find out what application is now active

At left end of menu bar, look at application name.

 —— *Active application*

Menus now contain Microsoft Word commands.

2 Switch applications by accident

Look at icons on desktop, to right of **Document1** window.

> *They were there when you started Microsoft Word. They don't belong to Microsoft Word, but you might click one by accident.*

Click desktop outside window. Look at application name now.

 —— *Active application*

> *Finder is active application. (Finder runs as soon as you start computer.) Menus now contain Finder commands.*

Notice faded Document1 window for Microsoft Word.

3 Switch back to Microsoft Word

Click anywhere on faded document window for Microsoft Word.

4 Hide Microsoft Word

On **Word** menu, choose **Hide Word**.

> *Word disappears from screen. Finder is now active application.*

5 Show Microsoft Word

On **Finder** menu, choose **Show All**.

Click faded document window for Microsoft Word.

> *Application name now appears on menu bar. Menu bar again contains commands for Microsoft Word application. Window is no longer faded.*

> *You can also bring back Microsoft Word by clicking its icon in dock.*

6 Avoid accidental window clicks

Make sure menu bar shows **Microsoft Word** as active application.

On **Word** menu, choose **Hide Others**.

> *Command hides all windows belonging to other applications. Now you can't click one by accident. (But watch out! Clicking desktop or item on desktop still makes Finder active.)*

Tip

When the computer isn't working the way it should, your first step should be to check the application icon and see what is active.

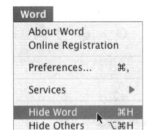

Tip

Whenever you start a program in the future, do step 6 here. With all other windows hidden, you won't easily click one accidentally.

Explore window

Information is always displayed in windows. You control the visibility, position, and size of windows.

1 **View Word Document1 window**

On menu bar, click **View**. If check is next to **Page Layout** on menu, close menu by clicking outside it. Otherwise, click **Page Layout**.

In this view, window shows page and start of text area on page. You'll learn about views on page 12.

Menu bar —
Standard toolbar —
Title bar —

Window contents —

Start of text area —

Vertical scroll bar —

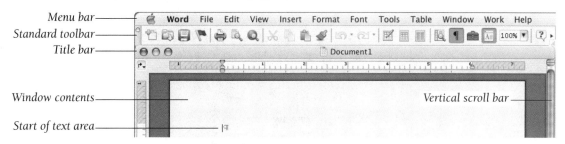

You may also see Formatting Palette *(dimmed) at right of window.*

2 **Close document window (method 1)**

On **File** menu, choose **Close**.

Window disappears; document is gone. If you changed document, Word will ask if you want to save changes. In dialog box, click Don't Save.

3 **Open new Word document (method 1)**

On **File** menu, choose **New Blank Document**.

New document named Document2 *appears in window.*

4 **Close document window (method 2)**

Move mouse pointer over buttons in upper left of title bar. Notice shapes.

Red close button contains **x***. Yellow minimize button contains* **-***. Green zoom button contains* **+***.*

At left of title bar, click red button at left 🔴🟡🟢 (close).

Window disappears; blank document is gone.

5 **Open new Word document (method 2)**

On standard toolbar, click 🗋 (new blank document).

New document named Document3 *appears in window.*

6 **Collapse (minimize) document window into dock (method 1)**

On **Window** menu, choose **Minimize Window**.

Window disappears, but Word menu bar and toolbar remain.

7 **Bring document back (method 1)**

On **Window** menu, choose **Document3**.

Window reappears.

8 *Collapse (minimize) window into dock (method 2)*

At left of title bar, click yellow button in middle  (minimize).

9 *Bring document back (method 2)*

In dock, click **Document3** icon.

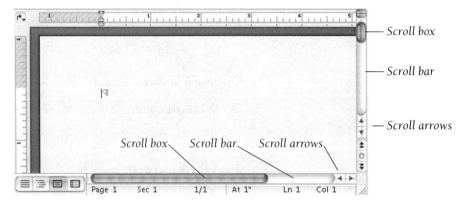

Document3 window reappears.

10 *Change window size*

Carefully move pointer to lower-right corner of window.

Hold mouse button down, and drag diagonally up and to left.

Release mouse button.

Window becomes smaller.

11 *Move window*

Put pointer inside title bar. Hold mouse button down, and drag window around screen.

Release mouse button.

Document window is in new location.

Try dragging window completely off left edge of screen.

You can't do that. Part of title bar always remains in view.

Drag window back in full view.

12 *View horizontal and vertical scroll bars*

Scroll boxes stand for portion of window contents now in view. Size of each scroll box shows what fraction of total is in view. You can see hidden contents by using features of each scroll bar.

By the way

If your computer has a small display screen, the initial window size may be smaller than shown in the figures in this book, and some tools may be missing from toolbars. You can enlarge the windows as shown in this activity.

13 *Use scroll arrows*

At right of horizontal scroll bar, watch window contents as you click ▶ (right scroll arrow). Repeat until motion stops.

> *Hidden contents of window "scrolls" into view from right. Scroll box moves to right, standing for new part now in view.*

At bottom of vertical scroll arrow, click ▼ (down scroll arrow). Repeat until motion stops.

Put pointer on ▲ (up scroll arrow). Press and hold mouse button down. Then release mouse button.

> *Effect is same as repeatedly clicking arrow.*

14 *Use scroll bar*

Click inside vertical scroll bar below scroll box. Repeat until motion stops.

> *Effect of each click is to move entire window contents out at top and bring same amount of new contents in at bottom.*

15 *Use scroll box*

Put pointer on scroll box in vertical scroll bar. Press and drag box slowly to top and back down.

Use both scroll boxes (or other method) to scroll back to top and left.

16 *Make window standard size (zoom); then restore it (method 1)*

On **Window** menu, choose **Zoom Window**.

> *Window becomes as tall as possible and has standard width.*

Choose **Zoom Window** again to zoom back to previous size.

17 *Make window standard size (zoom); then restore it (method 2)*

At left end of title bar, click green button at right ⊗⊖⊕ (zoom).

Click ⊗⊖⊕ again to zoom back to previous size.

18 *Change view scale*

Use either method to zoom window out to standard size.

At right end of toolbar, locate 100%▼ (zoom). Click ▼ to right of percent.

On pop-up menu, choose **75%** as zoom scale.

> *Window doesn't change size, but content is smaller.*

Use same method to choose **Whole Page** as zoom scale.

> *Percent changes as needed to fit page in window.*

Change view scale back to **100%**.

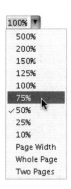

Tip

Don't confuse zooming the window with zooming the view scale. The first changes the size of the window; the second changes the size of what's inside the window.

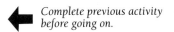

Complete previous activity before going on.

Explore view options

A Microsoft Office program begins in whatever view the last user left it. Here are ways to control the view of a document.

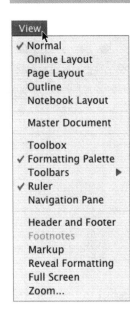

1 **Hide and show ruler**

See whether ruler appears just below title bar of **Document3** window.

On menu bar, click **View** to see menu.

Move pointer down menu to **Ruler**, and click it.

On **View** menu, choose **Ruler** again.

> *Command switches ruler on or off. Check mark means ruler is showing.*

If ruler is hidden now, repeat command once more.

2 **Set other options on menu as expected in this book**

On menu bar, click **View** to see menu.

Click items on menu as necessary so check marks appear as in figure at left.

> *In* Normal *view, page margins are hidden; text area fills window. You'll use* Formatting Palette *and* Ruler *often in this book.*

3 **See online layout view**

On **View** menu, choose **Online Layout**.

> *View is useful for creating Web pages using html code.*

4 **See page layout view**

On **View** menu, choose **Page Layout**.

> *View is useful for seeing how a document will look when printed.*

Tip

If the Formatting Palette covers an important area of your window, drag the palette by its title bar to a new location.

5 **See outline view**

On **View** menu, choose **Outline**.

> *View is useful for creating an outline—one way to start writing.*

6 **See notebook layout view**

On **View** menu, choose **Notebook Layout**.

> *View looks like school notebook, complete with tabs, date, and title.*

7 **Return to normal view**

On **View** menu, choose **Normal**.

> *If section breaks appear, ignore for now. You'll learn about them on page 61.*

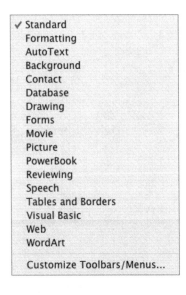

8 **Set up toolbars as expected in this book**

On **View** menu, put pointer on **Toolbars** to see submenu.

If **Standard** is not checked, click it. Look at **Toolbars** submenu again.

If any other submenu item *is* checked, click it to hide toolbar. Repeat until only **Standard** is checked.

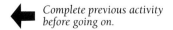
Set Word preferences

Preferences chosen by a previous user can change the way a program works. You'll set preferences expected in this book.

1 **Display Preferences dialog box**

On **Word** menu, choose **Preferences**.

> *Dialog box appears. Many categories are listed in left pane.*

Click each category, and look at options you can set. End at **View**.

Notice **Description of preference** at bottom when pointer is over item.

> *All* option under Nonprinting characters *is described in figure.*

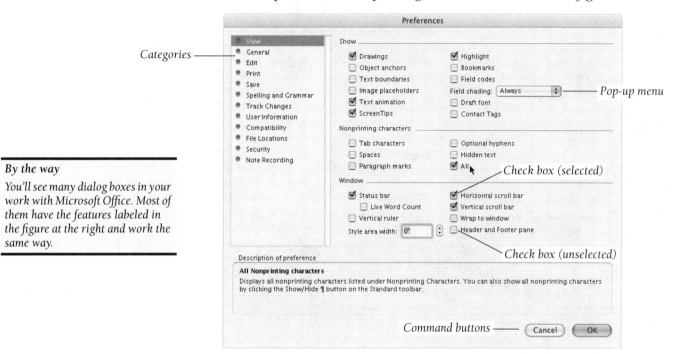

Categories —

Pop-up menu

Check box (selected)

Check box (unselected)

Command buttons — Cancel   OK

Description of preference

All Nonprinting characters
Displays all nonprinting characters listed under Nonprinting Characters. You can also show all nonprinting characters by clicking the Show/Hide ¶ button on the Standard toolbar.

By the way

You'll see many dialog boxes in your work with Microsoft Office. Most of them have the features labeled in the figure at the right and work the same way.

> *Each option affects some feature of program. To avoid surprises in this book, you'll set important options as expected.*

2 **Change options**

In **Show** area of **View** category, click **Highlight**. Click it again.

> *Option is "check box." Clicking switches check mark on or off.*

Locate pop-up menu labeled **Field shading**. Click 🔽 at right to see menu. Click any item on pop-up menu to choose it.

3 **Set view preferences expected in this book**

Click as necessary to make all check marks match figure at top of page. On **Field shading** pop-up menu, choose **Always**.

Carefully review each option before going on.

4 **Set general preferences**

In left pane, click **General**. Review options.

Remove check mark from **Show Project Gallery at startup**.

5   *Set editing preferences*

In left pane, click **Edit**. Review options, then make all match figure below.

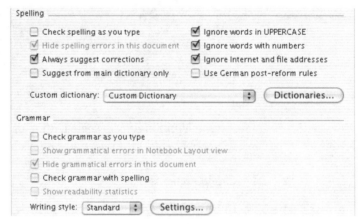

Editing options

- ☑ Typing replaces selection
- ☑ Drag-and-drop text editing
- ☑ Include paragraph mark when selecting paragraphs
- ☐ When selecting, automatically select entire word
- ☐ Use the INS key for paste
- ☐ Overtype mode
- ☑ Tabs and backspace set left indent
- ☐ Allow accented uppercase in French
- ☐ Keep track of formatting
- ☑ Match font with keyboard

Cut and paste options

- ☐ Show Paste Options buttons
- ☑ Use smart cut and paste   (Settings...)

Click and type (For current and future documents)

- ☐ Enable click and type   Default Paragraph Style: [Normal ⬍]

6   *Set spelling preferences*

In left pane, click **Spelling and Grammar**. Make all options match figure.

Spelling

- ☐ Check spelling as you type
- ☑ Hide spelling errors in this document
- ☑ Always suggest corrections
- ☐ Suggest from main dictionary only
- ☑ Ignore words in UPPERCASE
- ☑ Ignore words with numbers
- ☑ Ignore Internet and file addresses
- ☐ Use German post-reform rules

Custom dictionary: [Custom Dictionary ⬍]   (Dictionaries...)

Grammar

- ☐ Check grammar as you type
- ☐ Show grammatical errors in Notebook Layout view
- ☑ Hide grammatical errors in this document
- ☐ Check grammar with spelling
- ☐ Show readability statistics

Writing style: [Standard ⬍]   (Settings...)

At bottom of dialog box, click **OK** button to approve all changes.

7   *Switch off AutoCorrect options*

On **Tools** menu, choose **AutoCorrect**. Click names in bar at top to view different "pages" of dialog box.

On **AutoCorrect** page, switch off four options at top. On **AutoFormat As You Type** page, make sure five options at top are off. On **AutoText** page, switch off option at top. Click **OK**.

8   *Quit program, and shut down computer*

At bottom of **Word** menu, choose **Quit Word**. If asked whether to save, click **Don't Save**. Close any windows you see on desktop.

On Apple menu, choose **Shut Down**.

By the way

With AutoCorrect options switched off, what you type is what you'll see on the screen. As you gain experience, you may want to switch some options back on and see whether they are helpful in your work.

Tip

If in the future your program seems to be behaving strangely, check the Preferences and AutoCorrect dialog boxes. Some other user may have changed an option.

Start Microsoft Word

You are now ready to start the Microsoft Word application running on your computer.

IMPORTANT

Be sure you have chosen all Word preferences and other options on pages 12–14 before continuing.

1 Start computer (see page 2) and Microsoft Word (see page 7)

2 View document window for Word

If window is narrower than figure below, click [⊗ ⊖ ⊕] (zoom) to widen it.

If you see **Formatting Palette** on right or in other location, click [⊖] (close) at left of its title bar to put away for now.

Menu bar —
Standard toolbar —
Title bar —
Ruler —
Place to enter text —

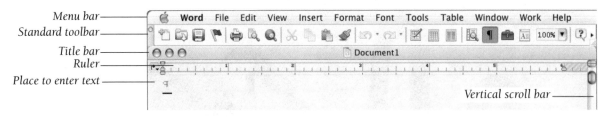

Vertical scroll bar —

3 Check toolbar and ruler

You can use commands on View menu to show and hide toolbar and ruler.

Place pointer over any icon on toolbar.

Name of tool appears below pointer.

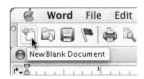

By the way

Toolbar icons are shortcuts for often-used menu commands. You get the same result whether you click the toolbar icon or choose the same command from a menu.

4 Check view settings

If you see wide margins at left and top of text entry area, choose **Normal** on **View** menu.

If view scale on zoom icon (at right of standard toolbar) is not **100%**, click tiny arrow at right.

On pop-up menu, choose **100%**.

This book is based on using default 100% view; if you wish, you may use different view percentage.

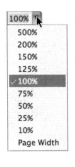

5 Check paragraph marks

If paragraph mark (¶) does not appear below ruler, click [¶] (show/hide ¶) on standard toolbar.

Special symbols will appear in text to show characters you type that are normally invisible: spaces, paragraph marks, and tabs. By making them visible, you'll see how they work, and you'll avoid adding or deleting one by accident.

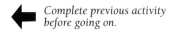

Complete previous activity before going on.

Create new document

Entering text into a new document is usually the first step in using a word processing program.

1 Locate insertion point

Look for small blinking vertical line to left of paragraph mark.

Insertion point is where characters will appear when you type.

2 Enter text

Type following text. Don't worry about typing errors now. You'll fix them later. Do *not* tap [RETURN] at ends of lines.

> **Today many people use very fast and powerful computers in business, at school, and at home. The computer revolution is the fastest-growing technology in recorded history.**

Insertion point moves as you enter text. Notice that words in paragraph automatically "wrap" (continue on next line when end of line is reached).

Tap [RETURN] now.

Look at insertion point and new paragraph mark.

Tapping [RETURN] marks end of paragraph, and moves insertion point to next line. Space characters appear as small dots.

3 Enter more text

Tap [RETURN] again to create blank line.

Another end-of-paragraph mark is visible on blank line.

Type following text. Ignore typing errors now.

> **It is easy to assume that computers are a recent addition to our lives. However, the start of the modern science that we call "computer science" can be traced back to the dust abacus, which was probably invented in Babylonia almost 5,000 years ago.**

Tap [RETURN] twice.

Tip

Type just one space between your sentences. Typing two spaces is a habit left over from the days of using a typewriter with fixed-width characters. The period was in the middle of a wide space, so extra space after it helped show that a new sentence was beginning.

By the way

If you see a red zigzag line under a misspelled word you type, the option to check spelling as you type has been switched on. Either ignore the mark or switch the option off (see page 14, step 6).

4   *Type following text; ignore typing errors now*

> Throughout the centuries, there have been many inventions and innovations that aided in the evolution of computer science. In the 1950s, two inventions dramatically changed the computer industry and caused the beginning of the "computer revolution."

Tap RETURN twice.

5   *Add your name to end of document*

Type your first and last names.

6   *Correct any error*

Move I-beam pointer just right of error, and click.

> *Insertion point appears where you clicked.*

Tap DELETE one or more times to remove characters.

> DELETE *is at upper-right corner of main group of keys.*

Enter correct characters.

Finished document should look like figure below.

Tip

You can also move the insertion point through a document by using the four arrow keys to the right of the main group of keys on keyboard.

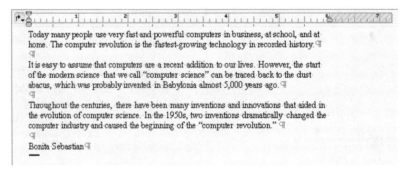

If you don't see paragraph marks, click ¶ on standard toolbar.

Complete previous activity before going on.

Save document

After creating and editing a new document, you should save it in a folder on your floppy disk, hard disk, or network.

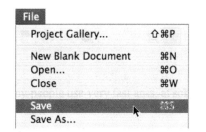

1 *Give Save command*

If you're using floppy disk, insert it in drive.

On **File** menu, choose **Save** (or click 🖫 on standard toolbar).

> Save As *sheet slides down from title bar on first use of* Save *command.*

2 *Name document*

Type `Computers` in highlighted part of **Save As** text box.

3 *Navigate to location where you want to save document*

If three panes in figure below do not appear on sheet, click 🔽 at right of **Save As** text box, to see paths to locations.

If using floppy disk, click **My Disk** in top part of left pane. In middle pane, click **My Files** folder with your initials.

Name of saved document ——
Place to save it ——
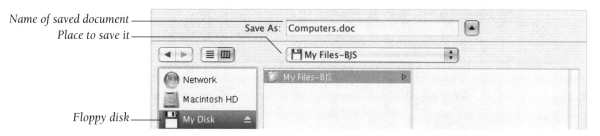
Floppy disk ——

Otherwise, click **Documents** in lower part of left pane. In middle pane, click **My Files** folder with your initials.

Name of saved document ——
Place to save it ——

By the way

If you or other people have previously logged in to the same user account and saved files, you will see other items in the middle pane.

Folder on hard disk ——

By the way

A file extension shows what application created the file: .doc for Word, .xls for Excel, etc. Macintosh applications don't need extensions to know the creator, but Windows applications do. If you add the extension, you can transfer a file to a Windows PC and continue working on it with the Windows version of the Microsoft Office application.

If necessary, click **Append file extension** check box to add **.doc** to document name. Click **Save** button. Notice new name in title bar.

4 *Add to document, and save again*

Click after **revolution.**" in last body paragraph. Tap spacebar

Type this: `The first was the transistor; the second was the integrated circuit or chip.`

On **File** menu, choose **Save** (or click 🖫 on standard toolbar).

> *No sheet slides down this time. Changed file takes place of original.*

← *Complete previous activity before going on.*

Save with new name

Often you need to save a changed document with a new name or in a new location so it won't erase the original.

1 **Add more text to document**

Click at end of your name.

Tap [RETURN] twice.

Type following addition:

> What do you think the future will bring to this exciting and fast-moving industry?

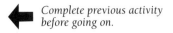

File	
Project Gallery...	⇧⌘P
New Blank Document	⌘N
Open...	⌘O
Close	⌘W
Save	⌘S
Save As...	
Save as Web Page...	

2 **Save changed document without erasing original**

If you're using floppy disk, be sure it's in drive.

On **File** menu, choose **Save As** (*not* Save; that would replace original).

> Save As *command makes* Save As *sheet slide down. It shows current name and current location of document. You can change either or both.*

In **Save As** text box, change name to **Revision**. Leave **.doc** extension.

Leave location as your **My Files** folder on floppy disk or in **Documents** folder.

New name ⎯⎯⎯
Same location ⎯⎯⎯

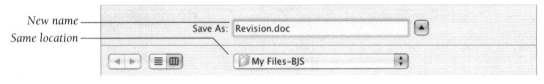

Save As: Revision.doc

My Files–BJS

Click **Save** button.

> *Now you have two documents saved. Computers has original text.* Revision *has original plus addition.*

Look at title bar of document window.

> *Title bar shows new document name. If you use* Save *command now, only new document is affected.*

3 **Close Computers document, quit Word, and shut down computer**

On **File** menu, choose **Close** (or click ⊗⊖⊕ at left of title bar).

On **Word** menu, choose **Quit Word**.

If you're using floppy disk and not continuing now, eject disk as shown on page 5, step 5.

On Apple menu, choose **Shut Down**.

By the way

If you close a document with changes you haven't yet saved, a dialog box asks whether you want to save the changes and offers three command buttons: Save is the same as giving the Save command before closing; Don't Save discards changes, and closes the document; Cancel stops the Close command and returns to the document. Choose Cancel if you want to be able to save the document with a new name; then choose Save As.

STOP Computers *file as saved on page 19 must be available.*

Open & print document

A document must be open for you to print it. You may need to select paper size and specify other things before printing.

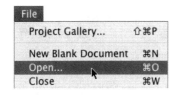

1 *Start computer (see page 2) and Microsoft Word (see page 7)*

2 *Locate document, and open it*

If you're using floppy disk, insert disk in drive. Wait for disk activity to end.

On **File** menu, choose **Open** (or click [icon] on standard toolbar).

> *Open dialog box appears. It's similar to* Save As *sheet. You navigate in same way to file you want to open.*

If using floppy disk, click **My Disk** in top part of left pane. In center pane, click **My Files** folder with your initials.

Place to look for saved files (folder on floppy disk)

Items saved at this location

Floppy disk

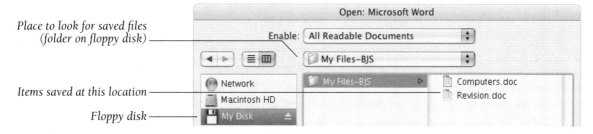

Otherwise, click **Documents** in bottom part of left pane. In center pane, click **My Files** folder with your initials.

Place to look for saved files (folder in Documents folder)

Items saved at this location

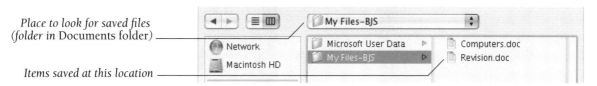

In either case, double-click **Computers** in list of saved files.

3 *Before printing, explore page setup options*

On **File** menu, choose **Page Setup**.

By the way

The Page Setup dialog box varies according to the printer and the printer driver software you are using.

Page Setup
Settings: Page Attributes
Format for: Any Printer
Paper Size: US Letter
8.50 in x 11.00 in
Orientation: [icons]
Scale: 100 %

4 *Select paper size and orientation of printed image on paper*

On **Paper Size** pop-up menu, choose size of paper now in printer. Click correct **Orientation** icon.

> *Left icon is vertical (portrait). Both right icons are horizontal (landscape).*

5 *Reduce or enlarge printed image (some printers)*

Type 90 in **Scale** text box (if present). Click **OK**.

6 *Check printer*

Is printer plugged in, and is switch on? Is paper in tray? Is cable from printer to computer inserted in proper computer port?

7 *Open Print dialog box*

On **File** menu, choose **Print**.

Dialog box varies according to printer and printer driver software you are using. Main features are same.

Tip
You can see other options for printing on the Copies & Pages *pop-up menu, including layout, output, paper handling, and color.*

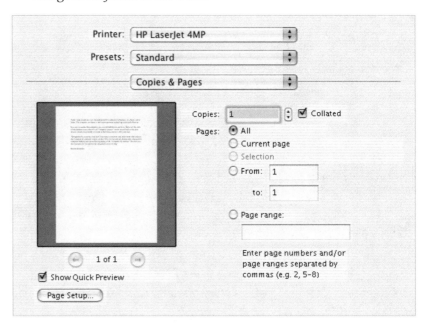

8 *Specify number of copies and range of pages*

Type 4 in **Copies** text box.

Tap TAB to go to **From** text box. Type 3 .

Tap TAB. Type 7 in **to** text box.

If you leave From *and* to *blank, all pages will be printed.*

By the way
You use the same methods to change printing options for graphics, presentation, spreadsheet, e-mail, and address book documents.

9 *Print one copy of whole document*

Change number of copies back to 1. Click **All** radio button.

Click **Print** button to start printing or **Cancel** if you don't want to print.

10 *Close Computers document without saving changes*

On **File** menu, choose **Close**. Click **Don't Save** if asked.

Select text

Text must be selected (highlighted) before you can make changes to it.

1 Open Computers document from your My Files folder (see page 21, step 2)

2 Select block of text (method 1)

Position I-beam pointer before first letter of first word you want to select.

With mouse button down, drag pointer through text you want to select.

You can drag horizontally or in any direction through text.

Release mouse button.

3 Deselect selected text

Click anywhere in text, or tap keyboard arrow key ($\downarrow$ or $\uparrow$ or $\rightarrow$ or $\leftarrow$).

Highlighting disappears. Insertion point appears where you clicked.

4 Select block of text (method 2)

Position I-beam pointer over first letter of first word you want to select. Click to place insertion point.

Hold down (SHIFT). Move pointer after last letter you want to select, then click. Release (SHIFT).

All text between places you clicked is selected.

5 Add to selected text

Hold down (SHIFT). Click after last letter you want added. Release (SHIFT).

Selection now extends from original starting place to last place clicked.

Click anywhere in text to deselect current selection.

By the way
You can add text to selection only in the same direction as before. You can remove text by clicking inside the selection.

6 Select block of text (method 3)

Put insertion point before first letter you want to select. Hold down (SHIFT) while you tap arrow keys.

Click anywhere in text to deselect current selection.

7 Select one word

Double-click any word.

Notice that space (but not punctuation) after word is also selected.

Deselect word.

8 Select one sentence

Tip
(⌘) keys are located to left and right of spacebar in main group of keys.

Hold down (⌘). Click anywhere in sentence.

Entire sentence, including period and space(s) after, is selected. Be careful: if you have any other text selected, effect is different (see step 12).

9 *Select one line of text*

Position pointer to left of any line of text.

> *Pointer shape changes to arrow leaning to right:* ↱ .

Click.

> *Entire line to right of pointer is selected.*

Click anywhere in text to deselect highlighted line.

10 *Select many lines of document*

Position pointer to left of first line you want to select.

Press mouse button and drag pointer down left side of document.

> *Highlighting follows pointer.*

Release mouse button.

Deselect highlighted area.

11 *Select paragraph*

Position pointer to left of paragraph, and double-click.

OR

Triple-click anywhere inside paragraph.

12 *Select nonadjacent text*

Select any single line of text.

Hold down ⌘ .

Select another line not adjacent to already selected line.

13 *Select entire document (method 1)*

Position pointer to left of all text. Triple-click.

Click anywhere in text to deselect it.

14 *Select entire document (method 2)*

On **Edit** menu, choose **Select All** (or hold down ⌘ , and tap Ⓐ).

> *Other menu commands often have "command key" shortcuts like this.*
> *(Hereafter, key combinations like this will appear as* ⌘ Ⓐ*.)*

15 *Deselect highlighted area.*

Click anywhere in text, or tap any keyboard arrow key.

16 *Close document without saving changes*

Use clipboard editing

After entering text, you often need to erase parts of it or move sentences and paragraphs around.

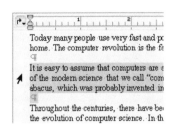

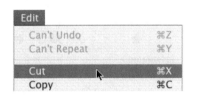

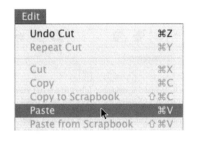

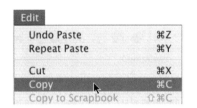

By the way

Cut or copied text is temporarily stored on the standard Macintosh clipboard for later use in the same or other documents or even in different programs. Cleared text is not placed on the clipboard.

1 **Open Computers document from your My Files folder (see page 21, step 2)**

2 **Select text paragraph 2**

Position pointer to left of first line in text paragraph 2.

Press and drag pointer down. Include blank line after paragraph.

3 **Cut selection to clipboard**

On **Edit** menu, choose **Cut** (or tap ⌘X, or click ✂ on toolbar).

> *Cut text is removed from document and stored on standard Macintosh clipboard. Using Cut (or Copy) again stores new text and deletes old.*

4 **Paste selection**

Click before first word in paragraph 1.

> *Blinking insertion point shows where cut text will be inserted. (If you accidentally selected whole line, repeat above step.)*

On **Edit** menu, choose **Paste** (or tap ⌘V, or click 📋 on toolbar).

> *Text is pasted from clipboard. Former text paragraph 2 is now paragraph 1.*

5 **Copy text**

Select text paragraph 3 and blank line after it.

On **Edit** menu, choose **Copy** (or tap ⌘C, or click 📋 on toolbar).

6 **Paste selection**

Click before first word in paragraph 1.

On **Edit** menu, choose **Paste** (or tap ⌘V, or click 📋 on toolbar).

7 **Delete new paragraph 1**

Select paragraph 1. Include blank line after it.

On **Edit** menu, choose **Clear**, then **Contents** (or tap DELETE).

8 **Add word**

Click before any word in any paragraph. Type `new` and tap spacebar.

9 **Delete word**

Double-click word **new**. Notice that word and space after are both selected.

Tap DELETE.

10 **Close Computers document without saving changes**

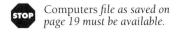

STOP Computers *file as saved on page 19 must be available.*

Use Scrapbook

The Microsoft Office Scrapbook allows you to copy and paste multiple pieces of text and objects among Office applications.

1 **Open Computers document from your My Files folder (see page 21, step 2)**

2 **View Scrapbook**

On **Tools** menu, choose **Scrapbook**.

3 **Copy selection to Scrapbook palette**

Select text paragraph 2 and blank line after it.

On **Edit** menu, choose **Copy to Scrapbook** (or tap (SHIFT)(⌘)(C)).

Copied text appears in Scrapbook *palette.*

4 **Paste from Scrapbook palette**

Click just before first word in paragraph 1 of document. On **Edit** menu, choose **Paste from Scrapbook** (or tap (SHIFT)(⌘)(V)).

Text on Scrapbook *palette (former paragraph 2) is copied into document. Text also remains available on palette.*

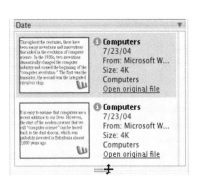

5 **Copy text to Scrapbook palette**

Select text paragraph 4 and blank line after it.

On **Edit** menu, choose **Copy to Scrapbook** or click ⊕ Add in palette.

New text appears in Scrapbook *palette above first.*

6 **Paste from Scrapbook into new document**

On standard toolbar, click 🔲 (new blank document).

On **Scrapbook** palette, click text at top. At bottom, click 📋 Paste .

Tip

If you cannot see the second text, press and drag the horizontal button at the bottom to enlarge the window. (See figure above.)

---

7 **Select and paste everything stored on Scrapbook palette**

Click first text on palette. Hold down (SHIFT), and click second text.

Click 📋 Paste .

Both pieces of selected text are pasted.

8 **Clear and close Scrapbook**

At bottom of **Scrapbook** palette, click tiny arrow at right of 🗑 Delete ▾ . On pop-up menu, click **Delete All**. In dialog box, click **Delete**.

Click ⊖ on palette title bar.

9 **Close both documents without saving changes**

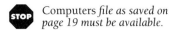
Use drag & drop editing

*Here's another way to move and duplicate text in a document.
Many people find it simpler and more direct.*

1 **Open Computers document from your My Files folder (see page 21, step 2)**

2 **Select text paragraph 2**

Position pointer to left of paragraph 2.

> *Pointer changes from I-beam shape to right-leaning arrow:* ↑ .

Double-click.

Tap (SHIFT ↓) to add blank line after paragraph to selection.

3 **Move selected paragraph 2 ahead of paragraph 1**

Notice pointer shape as you move it into any selected text. Do not click!

> *Instead of normal I-beam shape, pointer becomes left-leaning arrow.*

With pointer in selected text, hold down mouse button.

Drag arrow pointer just before first word in paragraph 1.

Notice that insertion point and dimmed image of text move with arrow.

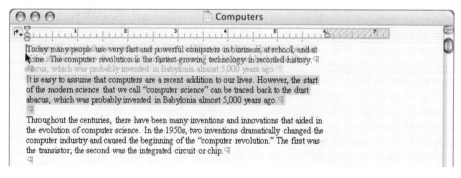

Release mouse button.

> *Selected text disappears from old location and is inserted at arrow position.
> You have dragged text paragraph 2 and dropped it before paragraph 1.*

4 **Place copy of paragraph 3 ahead of new paragraph 1**

Select text paragraph 3 and blank line after it.

Put pointer in selected text.

Hold down (OPTION) and mouse button.

Notice plus sign, which indicates you are copying, not moving, text.

Drag arrow pointer just before first word in new paragraph 1.

Release mouse button first, then (OPTION).

> *You have dragged copy of paragraph 3 and dropped it before paragraph 1.*

5 **Close Computers document without saving changes**

On **File** menu, choose **Close**.

Click **Don't Save** in dialog box.

By the way

*Drag-and-drop editing has no effect
on the clipboard or Scrapbook.*

Undo changes

Microsoft Word allows you to undo actions you have performed that changed the content or format of a document.

1 Open Computers document from your My Files folder (see page 21, step 2)

2 Select paragraph 1

Position pointer to left of paragraph 1. Notice pointer shape: ↗ .

Double-click right-leaning arrow.

3 Delete paragraph

On **Edit** menu, choose **Clear**, then **Contents**.

Paragraph is deleted.

4 Undo action (method 1)

On **Edit** menu, choose **Undo Clear** (or tap ⌘ Z).

Paragraph is "undeleted."

5 Delete paragraph again

With paragraph selected, tap (DELETE).

Paragraph is again deleted.

6 Undo action (method 2)

Click ↺ (undo) on standard toolbar.

Paragraph is again "undeleted."

7 Undo multiple actions

Click anywhere in text paragraph 1, and type AAAAA .

Click anywhere in text paragraph 2, and type BBBBB .

Click anywhere in text paragraph 3, and type CCCCC .

Click arrow at right of ↺· (undo).

Pop-up menu shows changes you've made. Most recent is at top, and rest are in order.

On undo pop-up menu, choose **Typing "AAAAA"**.

Effect is to undo all changes down through item you selected.

8 Redo changes just undone

On **Edit** menu, choose **Redo Typing** (or tap ⌘ Y or click ↻ if available).

You should again see AAAAA in paragraph 1, but not previous changes.

Repeat twice to see other changes reappear.

9 Close document without saving changes

Check spelling

Microsoft Word can check your words against its spelling dictionary and add new words to your custom dictionary.

1 **Open Computers document from your My Files folder (see page 21, step 2)**

Make sure spelling options are set as shown on page 14.

2 **Create spelling errors in text paragraphs 1 and 2**

Change *business* to *busness*. Change *revolution* to *revoluting*.

Change *recent* to *ricent*. Change *science* to *sciance*.

On new line after your name, type `Whoopdedoo`.

Put insertion point at start of document.

3 **Open Spelling dialog box**

On **Tools** menu, choose **Spelling and Grammar**.

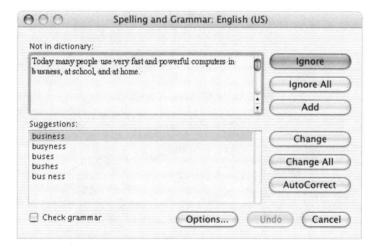

4 **Replace word not found in dictionary (method 1)**

In upper scroll box, notice "busness" in bold and red.

In **Suggestions** scroll box, notice that correct spelling is highlighted.

Click **Change**.

> *Clicking Change All would replace all similar misspellings in document.*

5 **View second word not in dictionary**

> *In upper scroll box, "revoluting" is next problem word. In Suggestions scroll box, word you want is not highlighted this time.*

6 **Replace word not found in dictionary (method 2)**

Double-click correct word in list (or click word, then click **Change**).

You can also check for and correct possible misspellings without using the Spelling and Grammar dialog box. First, switch on the option Check spelling as you type (see page 14, step 6). A red zigzag line appears under all doubtful words.

Tip

You can also check for and correct possible misspellings without using the Spelling and Grammar dialog box. First, switch on the option Check spelling as you type (see page 14, step 6). A red zigzag line appears under all doubtful words. Holding [CONTROL] *down, click a marked word to see a menu with suggested spellings and other options.*

By the way

If you had checked the Grammar options, you would have seen a Readability Statistics report. You close the report to go on.

7 Correct other words not in dictionary

Use either method to correct remaining words not found in dictionary.

If your name is flagged, click **Ignore All**.

> *Clicking* Ignore All *marks word as OK in document. It won't be flagged if you check this same document again.*

Stop at "Whoopdedoo."

8 Add unknown word to custom dictionary

> *"Whoopdedoo" is not in dictionary. You can add it, so it won't be flagged in this or other documents.*

Click **Add**.

> *Word adds "Whoopdedoo" to custom dictionary, which is shared with other Microsoft Office applications.*

When you are told that check is complete, click **OK**.

9 Remove word from dictionary

On **Word** menu, choose **Preferences**.

Click **Spelling and Grammar**.

Click **Dictionaries**. Click **Edit**.

> *Custom dictionary opens as Word document with words listed alphabetically in column.*

Locate, then select, and delete added word "Whoopdedoo."

10 Save and close custom dictionary document

On **File** menu, choose **Save**.

Click **Yes**.

On **File** menu, choose **Close**.

11 Close Computers document without saving changes

On **File** menu, choose **Close**.

Click **Don't Save** when asked whether to save.

STOP *Computers file as saved on page 19 must be available.*

Find text

You can get help in finding words you're looking for—a nice feature if your document has lots of text.

1 Open Computers document from your My Files folder (see page 21, step 2)

2 Set up document for finding special text

Capitalize words inside quotation marks in text paragraphs 2 and 3.

Move insertion point to beginning of text ([⌘][HOME] is shortcut).

Tip

If you're using a laptop computer, you must hold down the [FN] key to change the function of the arrow keys at the lower right to [HOME], [END], etc. For example, when you're told to tap [⌘][HOME], you should hold down [FN] as well as [⌘].

---

3 Find word

On **Edit** menu, choose **Find**. Type `Computer` in **Find what** box.

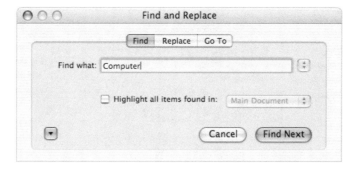

Click **Find Next** until search ends.

> *Text is found seven times before search ends. Notice that "computer" in "computers" was also found and that capitalization was ignored.*

Click **OK** to close dialog box that reports end of search.

4 Find whole word

At bottom left of dialog box, click ▼ to see additional search options.

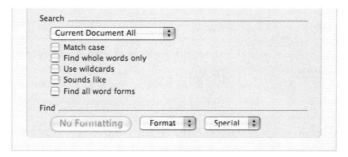

In **Search** area, click **Find whole words only** to put mark in check box.

Click **Find Next** until search ends. Click **OK**.

> *Only five matches are found now because you asked for only that exact word (and not others that contain "computer").*

Tip

The Find command is especially useful in long documents. It allows you to go directly to words or phrases anywhere in a document.

---

5 Make case-sensitive search

In **Search** area, click **Match case** check box. Click **Find Next**.

> *Whole word "Computer" with first letter capitalized is found twice.*

6 Click OK to end search; click Cancel to close dialog box

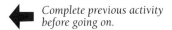
Replace text

Sometimes you need to change one word to another in many places in a document.

1 Begin replacement

Make sure insertion point is at start of document.

On **Edit** menu, choose **Replace** (or choose **Find**, and click **Replace** at top).

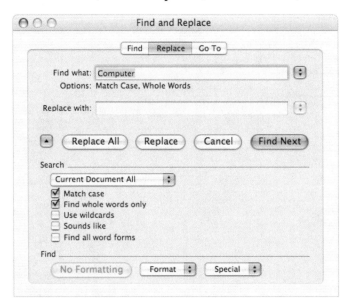

By the way

The last search text appears highlighted in the Find what box, and all check boxes are the way you left them.

2 Enter text to be replaced

Tap TAB. In **Replace with** box, type `abacus`. To remove marks, click **Match case** and **Find whole words only**.

3 Find and replace words one at a time

Click **Find Next**.

> *Word "computers" is highlighted.*

Click **Find Next** to avoid making change and go to next instance.

Click **Replace** to change "computer" to "abacus."

> *Next occurrence is word "computers," which you won't change.*

Click **Find Next**. Change each remaining occurrence of "computer."

Click **OK** to close message box reporting end of search.

By the way

Upper or lower case is matched when a word is replaced. "Computer" is replaced with "Abacus"; "computer" is replaced with "abacus."

4 Find and replace words without checking

Click to right of **Computer** in **Find what** text box. Type `s` and click **Replace All**.

> *Two instances of word "computers" are found and changed to "abacus."*

5 End Replace

Click **OK**, then click **Close** button.

6 Close Computers document without saving changes

STOP Computers *file as saved on page 19 must be available.*

Change fonts & sizes

Text can appear in many different fonts and sizes. Each font specifies the shapes of all the letters, numbers, and symbols.

1 **Open Computers document from your My Files folder (see page 21, step 2)**

2 **If necessary, open Formatting Palette**

On **View** menu, choose **Formatting Palette** or click  (formatting palette) on standard toolbar.

3 **Check current font and size of text in paragraph 1**

Select any text in paragraph 1.

In **Font** pane of **Formatting Palette**, look at **Name** and **Size** settings.

Palette shows name and size of font used for selected text.

4 **Change font**

In **Font** pane on **Formatting Palette**, click ▼ for **Name** pop-up menu.

Your list of fonts may be different but are in alphabetical order. Recent fonts used may be listed at top.

On **Name** pop-up menu, scroll up, and choose **Helvetica**.

Palette commands affect only selected text in document.

5 **Change size**

On **Formatting Palette**, click ▼ for **Size** pop-up menu. Choose **18**.

6 **Copy font style, and apply to other text**

With same text selected, click 🖌 (format painter) on standard toolbar.

Darkened tool means all formats of text have been copied.

Drag through any text in paragraph 2.

Formats are pasted on text you selected. Format painter tool is no longer darkened. (To paste formats more than once, you double-click tool; this keeps it darkened after pasting. When finished, you click tool once.)

7 **Change fonts and sizes, and save results**

Give words in each text paragraph different fonts and sizes.

On **File** menu, choose **Save As** (*not* Save).

Notice that location is same one you opened **Computers** document from.

Type Fonts in **Save As** text box.

Click **Save**.

Changed document is saved with new name. Original remains unchanged.

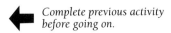
Apply font styles

You can easily add font styles, such as bold or italic, to selected text in a document.

1 **Add single style to all text in paragraph 2**

Select all of text paragraph 2.

On **Formatting Palette**, click **B** (bold), or tap ⌘ B on keyboard.

> *Selection appears in bold type. Notice that tool is outlined and darkened.*

2 **Remove same style**

On **Formatting Palette**, click **B**, or tap ⌘ B again.

> *Command is like on/off switch, so bold style is removed when you choose command again. Darkening and border on tool tell when it is on.*

3 **Add styles one at a time**

If necessary, select all text in paragraph 2.

On **Formatting Palette**, click **B**, or tap ⌘ B.

On **Formatting Palette**, click *I* (italic), or tap ⌘ I.

On **Formatting Palette**, click U (underline), or tap ⌘ U.

> *All three tools are darkened.*

Click outside text paragraph 2 to deselect text, and see styles.

> *Tools no longer have border or are darkened. That's because insertion point is not in text with those styles.*

Tip

You can also use the format painter tool (page 33, step 6) to copy font styles and paste them into other text. The format painter copies everything about the selected text— font, size, style, and color—and lets you paste the formats into other text.

4 **Remove added styles one at a time**

Select all text in paragraph 2.

Watch text as you click **B**, then *I*, then U.

5 **Undo last three actions**

On standard toolbar, click arrow at right of ↺ ▾ (undo).

On undo pop-up menu, choose *first* occurrence of **Bold**.

> *All three styles are added back to text.*

By the way

Tapping CTRL SPACEBAR *removes all applied character formats—font, size, style, and color. The effect is to return the selected text to its original appearance.*

6 **Remove applied styles**

With all text in paragraph 2 selected, tap CTRL SPACEBAR.

7 **Apply font styles, save, and close document**

Apply different styles to words in each text paragraph of document.

On **File** menu, choose **Save As** (*not* Save).

Type Styles in **Save As** text box. Click **Save**.

> *Changed document is saved in same location with new name.*

On **File** menu, choose **Close**.

STOP *Computers file as saved on page 19 must be available.*

Use Font dialog box

A single dialog box lets you specify all character formats at the same time: the font, the size, the styles, and other details.

WP / 35

1 **Open Computers document from your My Files folder**

2 **Change font, size, style, and color at same time**

Select all text in paragraph 1.

On **Format** menu, choose **Font**.

If necessary, click **Font** in bar near top.

Scroll bar arrows ——

Use scroll bar arrows on **Font** list to see fonts. Click to select one you want.

On **Font style** list, click **Bold Italic**.

On this list, Regular *means no italic, no bold.*

Use scroll bar on **Size** list to see sizes. Click to select one you want.

On **Font color** pop-up menu, choose dark red.

On **Underline style** pop-up menu, click first single line.

In **Effects** area, click **All caps** to put mark in check box.

Click **OK**. Then click away from paragraph 1 to see result.

All changes happen at same time.

3 **Remove all character formats you've applied**

Select all text in paragraph 1. Tap CTRL SPACEBAR.

4 **Close document without saving changes**

At least two Word documents must be available.

Open multiple documents

In Word, like most Macintosh applications, you can have several documents open in separate windows.

1 **Open multiple documents**

Use procedure on page 21, step 2, to reach your **My Files** folder, but don't open any document yet.

Open dialog box should look like one or other figure on page 21, but with more document names in right pane.

Click name of first document in list.

With (⌘) held down, click one or more other names in list.

Document names become highlighted.

Click **Open**.

All documents open, but only last document is visible.

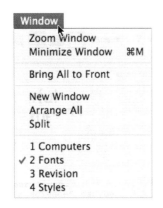

2 **Switch from document to document**

On **Window** menu, at bottom, choose unchecked document name.

Document window comes in front, covering others.

3 **View all documents at one time**

On **Window** menu, choose **Arrange All**.

All windows are visible and fill desktop below toolbar. Only one is active (notice title bars).

4 **Activate different window**

Click anywhere in inactive window to activate it.

5 **Zoom windows to standard size**

In upper-left corner of active window, click ⊗⊖⊕ (zoom).

Click ⊗⊖⊕ again to zoom back in to previous size. Zoom out again.

Use **Window** menu to activate another window. Zoom out.

Repeat until all windows have standard size.

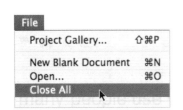

6 **Close multiple documents**

Press (SHIFT), and hold it down.

On **File** menu, choose **Close All**.

If asked, don't save changes.

7 **Quit Microsoft Word**

On **Word** menu, choose **Quit Word**.

If you're using floppy disk and not continuing now, eject disk as shown on page 5, step 5.

Align text

The lines of text in a paragraph can all be aligned to the left, the right, the center, or both the left and the right (justified).

1 Start Microsoft Word

If necessary, open **Formatting Palette**

2 View paragraph formatting tools on Formatting Palette

On palette, click **Alignment and Spacing** bar.

> *Pane appears. You'll use most tools here in next three activities.*

3 Enter text using alignment options

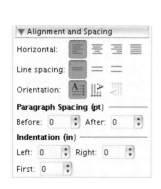

In **Horizontal** group at top of pane, click ☰ (align center).

> *Insertion point moves to center of document. Tool is outlined and darkened.*

Type Computer History Society .

Tap RETURN twice.

> *Each new line picks up previous center-alignment formatting.*

In same group, click ☰ (align right).

> *Insertion point moves to right. New tool is outlined and darkened.*

4 Enter automatic date

On **Insert** menu, choose **Date and Time**.

On **Available formats** list, choose format you like. Click **OK**.

Tip

The **Update automatically** *option means that each time you open the document, the date and time will change to reflect the current date and time. If you do not want the date and/or time to change, remove the check mark.*

5 Enter additional text with left alignment

Tap RETURN twice.

> *Each new line picks up previous right-alignment formatting.*

In **Horizontal** group, click ☰ (align left).

> *Insertion point moves to left side of document.*

Type Mr. John Smith, .

---

6   *Add blank lines*

Tap `RETURN` twice.

> *Each new line picks up previous left-alignment formatting.*

7   *Enter body paragraph*

Type following paragraph. Do not tap `RETURN` at ends of lines. Let text wrap.

> How many times have you wondered about the history of computers or about the "computer revolution"? Is this a modern phenomenon or simply another step in the evolution of technology? The Computer History Society meetings offer thought-provoking discussions on such topics. Please join us next month.

8   *Change left alignment to justified alignment*

Click anywhere in body paragraph to select it.

> *Alignment commands (and all other paragraph format commands) affect paragraph with insertion point or with any selected text.*

In **Alignment and Spacing** pane of **Formatting Palette**, click ▤ (justify).

Notice ends of lines.

> *Text has even (justified) right and left margins.*

9   *Copy and paste paragraph format*

Click anywhere in centered title. Do *not* highlight any text.

Click 🖌 (format painter) on standard toolbar.

> *Darkened tool means format of paragraph has been copied.*

Click anywhere in paragraph with date.

> *Centered-text format is pasted on paragraph you clicked. Format painter tool is no longer darkened*

10   *Save document*

If using floppy disk, make sure it's inserted. Wait until drive activity stops.

On **File** menu, choose **Save**.

In **Save As** text box, type `CHSNote`.

If necessary, navigate to your **My Files folder**. Click **Save**.

11   *Move insertion point to top of document*

Tap `⌘ HOME` (or `FN ⌘ HOME` if you're using laptop).

By the way

If any text is highlighted, the format painter copies the font format. If nothing is highlighted, the format painter copies the paragraph format of the paragraph with the insertion point.

← *Complete previous activity before going on.*

Apply indents

Other paragraph format controls let you indent lines in paragraphs from the left and right margins.

1 *View indent markers at ends of ruler*

If ruler is not present, choose **Ruler** on **View** menu.

First-line indent ——
Left indent ——

—— *Right indent*

2 *Set right and left indents*

Click anywhere inside body paragraph.

> *Paragraph formatting applies to paragraph where insertion point is located. You don't have to select entire paragraph.*

Press and drag right indent marker 2 inches to left (to 4" mark on ruler).

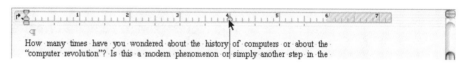

How many times have you wondered about the history of computers or about the "computer revolution"? Is this a modern phenomenon or simply another step in the

> *Text is indented from right margin in selected paragraph (one with insertion point in it) only. To set indents in more than one paragraph, select some text in each.*

Press and drag rectangular left indent marker 1 inch to right (to 1" mark on ruler).

> *Dragging left indent marker also moves first-line indent marker.*

On **Formatting Palette**, look at **Indentation** numbers.

> *You can also change indents by entering numbers here. Markers will move.*

Tip

If the ruler units are not inches, you can switch units on the Word menu, Preferences dialog box, General pane, Measurement units pop-up menu.

3 *Set first-line indent*

Carefully press and drag first-line indent marker (*top* triangle, now above left indent marker) to right ½ inch (to 1.5" mark).

> *This time, first line of selected paragraph is indented more than rest.*

4 *Set hanging indent*

Carefully press and drag first-line indent marker (*top* triangle) to left 1 inch (to 0.5" mark).

> *This time, first line "hangs"—begins to left of other lines. Format is useful for numbered or bulleted paragraphs.*

Notice **Indentation** numbers on **Formatting Palette** now.

Warning!

Be careful not to drag too far to the left and into the "minus area." If you do, use the horizontal scroll bar at the bottom of the window to locate the markers, and drag them back.

5 *Return indents to original settings*

If necessary, click in body paragraph again.

> *You could drag markers to original positions, but it's simpler now just to remove all paragraph formatting you've applied.*

Tap ⌘ SHIFT N to return to normal paragraph format.

Apply line spacing

Additional paragraph format controls let you change vertical line spacing.

1 **Select paragraph to be affected**

If necessary, click inside body paragraph.

Like alignment and indentation, line spacing affects only paragraph with insertion point (or paragraphs with some text selected).

2 **Change line spacing (method 1)**

In **Alignment and Spacing** pane of **Formatting Palette**, locate three **Line spacing** buttons.

Watch body paragraph as you click ═ (double space), then ═ (1.5 space), then ═ (single space).

3 **Change line spacing (method 2)**

Watch body paragraph and **Formatting Palette** as you tap ⌘ 2 .

Lines are double-spaced now.

Tap ⌘ 5 for 1.5 line spacing. Tap ⌘ 1 for single spacing.

4 **Remove blank line before body paragraph**

Put insertion point at start of body paragraph.

Tap DELETE to remove any blank lines before paragraph.

Now you'll learn another way to put space between paragraphs.

5 **Add space before paragraph (method 1)**

Click inside body paragraph.

On **Formatting Palette**, locate two **Paragraph Spacing** text boxes.

At right of **Before** text box, click tiny up-arrow twice to make number **12**.

Units are points (pt); 72 pt equals 1 inch.

Notice that there's no paragraph mark on space before body paragraph.

Double-click arrow pointer just left of body paragraph to select it.

Blank line is also selected. It's part of paragraph format now.

At right of **Before** text box, click tiny down-arrow twice so number is **0**.

By the way

You can use the format painter tool (see page 38, step 9) to copy all paragraph formats—alignment, indentation, spacing, tab stops, numbering—in one paragraph, and paste them into other paragraphs.

6 **Add space before paragraph (method 2)**

Tap ⌘ 0 (zero) to add one line space. Look at number in **Before** box.

One line space is added before selected paragraph.

With body paragraph still selected, tap ⌘ 0 (zero) again.

Line space goes away.

7 **Close document without saving changes**

STOP Computers *file as saved on page 19 must be available.*

Use Paragraph dialog box

Like the Font *dialog box, this one lets you make many format changes at the same time. They affect whole paragraphs.*

1 **Open Computers document from your My Files folder**

2 **Delete blank lines between text paragraphs**

Move pointer to left side of document.

> *Pointer changes to right-leaning arrow: ⬈ .*

Click to left of first blank line after text paragraph 1. Tap DELETE.

Do same for blank lines after text paragraphs 2 and 3).

3 **Select some text in all three body paragraphs**

Click anywhere in paragraph 1. With SHIFT held down, click anywhere in paragraph 3.

4 **Open Paragraph dialog box**

On **Format** menu, choose **Paragraph**.

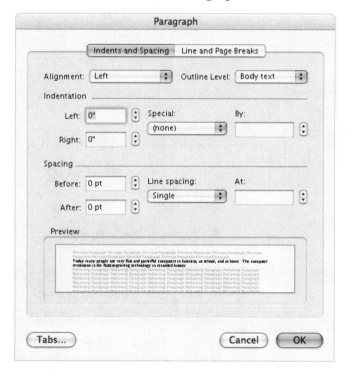

On **Alignment** pop-up menu, choose **Justified**.

In **Indentation** area, on **Special** pop-up menu, choose **First line**. In **By** box, choose **0.5"** if necessary.

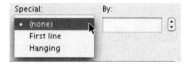

In **Spacing** area, in **After** box, click up-arrow twice to choose **12 pt**.

On **Line spacing** pop-up menu, choose **1.5 lines**.

Click **OK**.

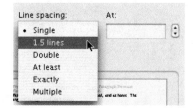

> *All format changes happen at once. Only paragraphs 1–3 are affected.*

5 **Close document without saving changes**

Use tab stops

Tab stops are another paragraph format feature. They give you control over alignment of words in columns.

1 Create new document (unless you just started Word)

On standard toolbar, click 🗋 (new blank document).

2 Notice tab features on ruler

If ruler is not present, choose Ruler *on* View *menu.*

Tab stop tool ⟶
Default tab stops ⟶

Default tab stops every ¹/₂ inch are in effect until you place your own stops.

At left of ruler, click tiny down arrow to view pop-up menu of tab stops.

With **Left** selected, click away from menu to close it.

3 Set custom tab stops (method 1)

With tab stop tool set to **Left**, click ruler at 0.75" mark.

Left tab stop appears where you clicked on ruler. Default tab stop to left of custom tab stop disappears. Default stops to right remain.

On tab stop menu, choose **Right**.

Click ruler at 2.5".

Use same steps to set decimal tab at 3.5" and center tab at 5".

Ruler should look like this:

Tab format applies to paragraph with insertion point (now blank).

4 Use tab stops

Using ⌜TAB⌝ (at left side of keyboard), type this:

⌜TAB⌝ Left ⌜TAB⌝ Right ⌜TAB⌝ 3.0 ⌜TAB⌝ Center ⌜RETURN⌝

You see arrow each place you tap ⌜TAB⌝. *(If not, click* ¶ *on standard toolbar to make nonprinting characters visible.)*

Notice where insertion point is. Look at stops in ruler now.

Insertion point is in new paragraph with same tab stops. Whenever you tap ⌜RETURN⌝, *new paragraph "inherits" tab stops (and all other formats) from previous one.*

Type this in new paragraph:

⌜TAB⌝ Apple ⌜TAB⌝ IBM ⌜TAB⌝ $999.98 ⌜TAB⌝ Dell

Words and numbers align with ones above.

5   *Clear all tab stops from new paragraph*

Tap (RETURN) twice to add blank line.

> *As before, same tab stops are inherited by new paragraph.*

Press and drag left tab stop (at 0.75") down from ruler. Release mouse button.

Do same for other tab stops on ruler.

> *New line has default tab stops but no custom tab stops. Custom tab stops remain in paragraphs above. Each paragraph has its own format settings.*

6   *Set custom tab stops (method 2)*

On **Format** menu, choose **Tabs**.

By the way

You can also open this dialog box by selecting Tabs *from the tab stop pop-up menu.*

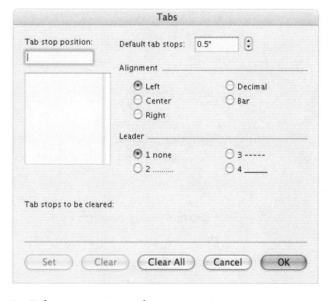

In **Tab stop position** box, type 1 .

Click **Set** button at bottom.

In **Tab stop position** box, type 5 .

In **Alignment** area, click **Decimal**.

Click **Set**, then **OK**.

7   *Use tab stops*

Type these lines:

> (TAB) Dell (TAB) 962.59 (RETURN)
> (TAB) Apple (TAB) 1896.95 (RETURN)
> (TAB) Sony (TAB) 1993.98 (RETURN)

> *Each new paragraph gets tab stops from previous paragraph.*

8   *Close document without saving changes*

Use tab leaders

When you use a tab stop, you can easily put a row of dots, dashes, or underlines in the space before the tab stop.

1 **Create new blank document (unless you just started Word)**

2 **Create single tab stop with leader**

On **Format** menu, choose **Tabs**. Duplicate **Tabs** dialog box below:

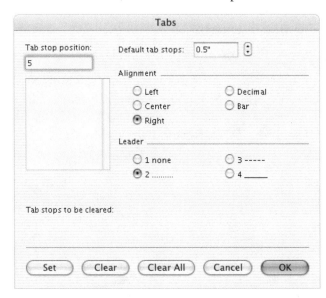

It sets one right tab stop at 5" mark with leader number 2 (dotted). Settings affect blank paragraph with insertion point.

Click **OK**.

3 **Enter two lines using new tab stop**

Chapter 1 `TAB` 1 `RETURN`
Chapter 2 `TAB` 12 `RETURN`

4 **Use different types of tab leaders**

On Ruler, double-click tab stop at 5" mark.

Tabs dialog box opens. Tab at 5 inches should be selected. If not, click tab on ruler to select it.

Under **Leader**, choose **3** (dashed line). Click **OK**, and type as follows.

Chapter 3 `TAB` 25 `RETURN`

Use same methods to complete figure below.

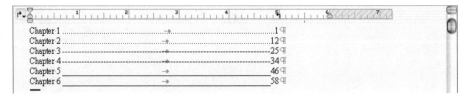

> **Tip**
>
> *Tab stop icons are tiny, so you must be careful not to move the mouse when you double-click. If all else fails, use the method in step 2 to open the Tabs dialog box.*

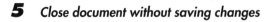

5 **Close document without saving changes**

Use bullets & numbering

You can add bullets and numbering to text to enhance visual interest and clarity. Each is added as a paragraph feature.

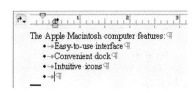

1 *Create new blank document (unless you just started Word)*

2 *Add text*

Type The Apple Macintosh computer features: and tap [RETURN].

3 *Add paragraphs with bullets*

On **Formatting Palette**, click **Bullets and Numbering**, if necessary, to see pane. If you need space, click other pane titles to close panes.

In **Bullets and Numbering** pane, click ▦ (bullets).

> *Empty paragraph is indented; bullet and tab are added.*

Enter text in figure to left. Notice that bullet format continues in next paragraph when you tap [RETURN].

4 *Turn off bullets, and add blank line*

Click ▦ (bullets), then tap [RETURN].

5 *Change format of bullets*

Select lines with bulleted text. On **Format** menu, choose **Bullets and Numbering**. Select different bullet style. Click **OK**.

6 *Add numbered text*

Tap [⌘] [END] (or [FN] [⌘] [END] if using laptop) to move to end of document.

Type To access the computer lab: and tap [RETURN].

In **Bullets and Numbering** pane of **Formatting Palette**, click ▦ (numbering). Notice that number, indent, and tab are added.

Type numbered list in figure below.

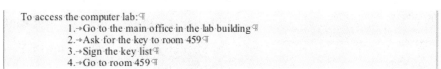

7 *Turn off numbering, and add text*

Tap [RETURN]. In **Bullets and Numbering** pane of **Formatting Palette**, click numbering button.

Type Don't forget to return the key!.

> To access the computer lab: ¶
>   1.→Go to the main office in the lab building ¶
>   2.→Ask for the key to room 459 ¶
>   3.→Sign the key list ¶
>   4.→Go to room 459 ¶
> Don't forget to return the key! ¶

8 *Close document without saving changes*

Tip

You can change the format of numbers in a list. On the Bullets and Numbering *pane of the* Formatting Palette, *click the* Style *pop-up menu.*

You can also change the Start *number in the text box at the right.*

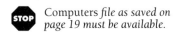 Computers *file as saved on page 19 must be available.*

By the way

Using named styles for all paragraphs in a document has two benefits. First, it makes headings and body paragraphs consistent throughout the document. Second, if you change the definition of a style, all paragraphs with that named style are automatically updated.

By the way

You can make all these changes on the Formatting Palette if you prefer.

Define paragraph styles

You can give a name to any combination of paragraph (or character) formats. Then you can apply the formats by name.

1 **Open Computers document from your My Files folder**

2 **See current styles in document**

On **Formatting Palette**, click **Styles** bar to see pane.

Every new document you create comes with these named styles.

Notice **Current style of selected text** (Normal).

This is style of paragraph with insertion point.

3 **Apply named style to selected paragraph**

Click anywhere in text paragraph 2.

On palette, in **Pick style to apply** list, click **Heading 1**.

Notice changes in text. Whole paragraph is affected.

Click anywhere in text paragraph 3. On palette, in **Pick style to apply** list, click **Heading 2**.

4 **Remove applied styles**

With ⇧SHIFT held down, click anywhere in paragraph 2.

Some text should be selected in paragraphs 2 and 3.

On palette, in **Pick style to apply** list, scroll down if necessary, and click **Normal** (or tap ⌘ SHIFT N).

Both paragraphs return to original formatting.

5 **Apply formats, one at a time, to paragraph 1**

Click anywhere in paragraph 1.

On **Format** menu, choose **Paragraph**.

In **Indentation** area, set **Left** and **Right** to 1".

On **Special** pop-up menu, choose **First line**. Leave **0.5"** in **By** text box. On **Line spacing** pop-up menu, choose **1.5 lines**.

Click **OK** to see result.

Paragraph 1 should have all formats just defined for it. Next, you'll create named style that does whole job with single click.

6 **Create new style based on current paragraph formatting**

In **Formatting Palette**, below current style, click New Style... .

7 *Name style, and apply it*

Type Indented and click **OK**.

Style named Indented *is created, using formats from current paragraph.*

With insertion point still in paragraph 1, click **Indented** in list of styles.

Click in paragraph 3. Click **Indented** in list of styles.

8 *View style name of each paragraph*

In **Style** pane, watch style name at top as you click each text paragraph.

Paragraphs 1 and 3 have Indented *style; rest have* Normal *style.*

9 *Change definition of Indented style*

On **Pick style to apply** list, put pointer at **Indented**. Click arrow at right.

Pop-up menu appears below Indented *(and arrow disappears).*

On pop-up menu, choose **Modify Style**.

Modify Style *dialog box is similar to* New Style *dialog.*

At lower left, click **Format** to see complete list of features you could change. Click again to hide list.

You'll make changes from options already in dialog box.

In **Formatting** area of **Modify Style** dialog box, click *I* and =.

Area should look like figure below.

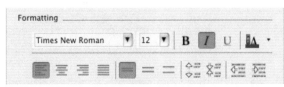

Click **OK**.

New definition is automatically applied to both paragraphs with Indented *style. Using named styles makes it easy to change your mind about formats.*

10 *Close document without saving changes*

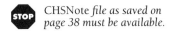
Add graphic object

You can add a graphic object to a word processing document. Microsoft Word contains a gallery of clip art you can use.

1 Open CHSNote document from your My Files folder

2 Insert graphic object

Make sure insertion point is at left of **Computer History Society**.

On **Formatting Palette**, click **Add Objects** bar to open pane.

In **Graphics** group, click  (insert clip art).

> Clip Gallery *appears.*

In **Search** box, type computer ; click **Search** button. Click image you like. Click **Insert**.

> *Picture is inserted next to title.*

If necessary, click picture to select it. With picture selected, notice many new options on **Formatting Palette** for modifying graphics.

3 Adjust size of object

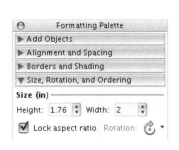

In **Size, Rotation, and Ordering** pane, in **Height** box, type 1 and tap TAB. Notice that **Width** automatically changes.

> *Because* Lock aspect ratio *is checked, width automatically adjusts to maintain object's ratio of height to width (keeps proportions same).*

4 Put object into separate (empty) paragraph

Move insertion point between picture and word "Computer." Tap RETURN to create new paragraph.

> *Picture is centered on page above title.*

5 Close document, saving changes when asked

Use AutoText entries

Microsoft Word has built-in text entries you can use to speed up
document creation. You can also create your own entries.

1 **Create new blank document (unless you just started Word)**

2 **Switch AutoText feature on**

On **View** menu, choose **Toolbars**, then **AutoText**.

If toolbar is docked at top (or other edge) of window, put pointer on bar at
left, and drag toolbar to middle of window.

At left of AutoText toolbar, click ![autotext icon] (autotext) to see options.

If check box at top is empty, click it.

By the way

*You can also reach the dialog box at
the right by choosing AutoCorrect
on the Tools menu or AutoText on
the Insert menu. It's the same dialog
box, no matter how you reach it.*

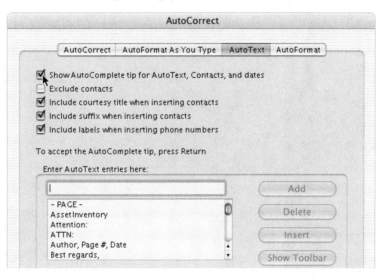

Scroll down through list to view collection of AutoText phrases (may vary).

You'll soon see what they can do to save typing effort.

Click **OK** to enable AutoText and close dialog box.

3 **Explore AutoText feature**

Type `best` and one space.

So far, nothing is new.

Type `r` and look at box just above line of type.

Box has tip suggesting phrase you may want.

Tap RETURN to replace your typing with tip.

If tip was not what you wanted, you'd just keep on typing as usual.

Tap RETURN to start new line. Type `atte` and tap RETURN to accept tip.

On same line, type one space. Type `atte` again.

*Oops! There's no tip this time. AutoText is smart enough to know that "atte"
can't mean "Attention:" unless it's at start of line.*

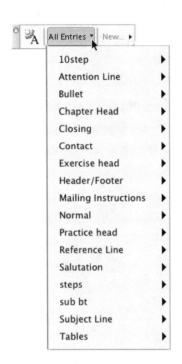

4 **Insert AutoText entry manually**

Tap [RETURN] to start new line.

On AutoText toolbar, click **All Entries** to view pop-up menu.

On pop-up menu, point to **Closing**. Click entry you like.

> *Text is inserted in document at insertion point.*

5 **Create custom AutoText entry**

Tap [RETURN] to move to blank line in document.

Type Computer History Society.

Select and format text as 16 point, bold.

If necessary, select whole line, including paragraph mark at end.

> *Paragraph mark will include formatting in AutoText item.*

On AutoText toolbar, click New... ▶.

Type chsoc and click **OK** to add name to list.

By the way

The name you use must be at least four characters in length for the AutoText feature to work.

---

6 **View new AutoText item**

On **All Entries** pop-up menu on toolbar, point to **Normal**.

> *New entry you created appears here.*

7 **Insert custom AutoText in document**

Click to right of first line of document, and type one space.

Type chsoc and notice tip above typing. Tap [RETURN] to insert formatted AutoText entry.

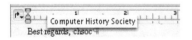

8 **Delete AutoText item from list**

At left of AutoText toolbar, click [A] (AutoText) to see options.

Scroll down in list. Click **chsoc**. Click **Delete**. Click **OK** to close **AutoCorrect** dialog box and save change.

9 **Disable AutoText feature**

On toolbar, click [A]. Click check box at top. Click **OK** to disable feature.

10 **Close AutoText toolbar; close document without saving changes**

Use Project Gallery

Microsoft Word has many formatted templates and wizards
that make it easy for you to create useful documents.

File
Project Gallery... ⇧⌘P

1 **Create new document using Project Gallery**

If necessary, start Word.

On **File** menu, choose **Project Gallery**.

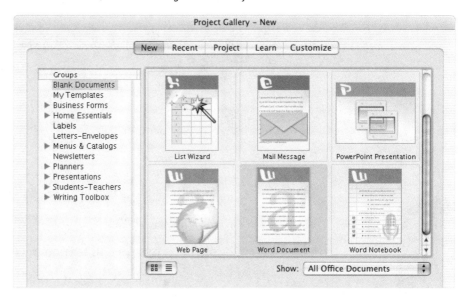

In **Groups** list, click triangle to left of **Business Forms**. Click **Fax Covers**.

Click one you like; click **Open**.

> *Fax cover template appears with text placeholders.*

2 **Enter text**

On **View** menu, choose **Zoom**. In **Zoom to** area, increase percentage to view you like. Click **OK**.

Click text blocks (may vary), and enter text:

Send to:	Sally Petersen	From:	(Type your name)
Attention:	All Department Heads	Date:	(Type current date)

Add text in other blocks if you want.

In **Comments** section, type:

> The Microsoft Word training will be held in the Computer Training Center on Tuesday, March 14. Please let me know how many people from your department will be attending.

3 **Save, print, and close fax cover**

If using floppy disk, make sure it's inserted now.

On **File** menu, choose **Save**. Name file FaxCover1. Navigate to your usual location for saving. Click **Save**.

Print fax cover if you like (see page 21).

On **File** menu, choose **Close**.

By the way

The fax cover opens in page layout view, where you can see the background graphics and the edges of the page. This view of the document shows more than the normal view, but it can be slower to work with.

Use notebook layout

Notebook layout makes it easy for you to take and organize separate sets of notes for different classes or meetings.

1 Create new blank document (unless you just started Word)

2 Switch to notebook layout

On **View** menu, choose **Notebook Layout**.

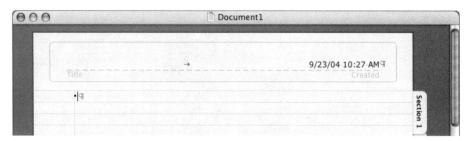

View has box at top for title and automatic date and time stamp, place below for notes, and tabs on right for different sections (white one is selected).

3 Organize notebook file

Double-click to select all text on **Section 1** tab. Type `Computers`.

Change **Section 2** tab name to "English." Change **Section 3** tab to "Math."

Click plus sign below tabs to create tab for new section.

Change **Section 4** tab to "History."

To delete tab, you need to hold down CONTROL *as you click tab; then choose Delete Section on pop-up menu. Any text in that section is also deleted.*

Click **English** tab. Drag it down until small triangle is below **Math**.

You move tabs by dragging them. Any text in section follows tab.

4 Add title to first section

Click **Computers** tab to activate first section.

Click **Title** in box at top, and type `History of Computers`.

5 Make notes (as if at lecture on subject)

Type text in figure below. To indent and "undent" lines, use ⊞ Demote and ⊟ Promote in **Note Levels** pane of **Formatting Palette**.

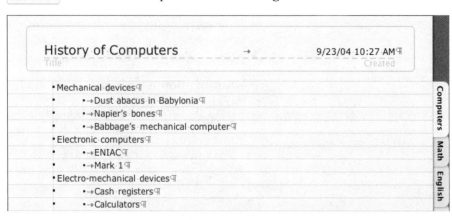

Tip

You can also use TAB *and* SHIFT TAB *to change indentation of the outline without having to switch between the keyboard and the mouse.*

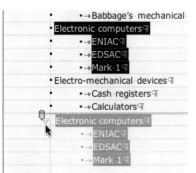

6 Modify notes (as if going over notes later)

Add item: Click to right of **ENIAC**, and tap RETURN. Type EDSAC.

New item is at same level as previous one. (You could demote or promote it.)

Move item: Put pointer to left of **Electronic Computers**. Press and drag blue triangle down so gray line is below **Calculators**. Release mouse button.

Subheadings move along with item you moved, and all remain selected.

Collapse and expand item with subheads: Move pointer to left of **Electro-mechanical devices**. Click small blue triangle. Click it again.

7 Scribble over text

On standard toolbar that appears in Notebook Layout, put pointer over each tool, and read description.

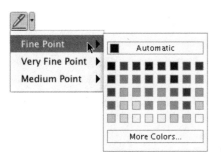

On toolbar, click tiny arrow at right of (scribble). On pop-up menu, choose point thickness, then color you want.

Press and drag using scribble tool to draw mark, as in figure at left.

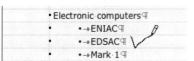

8 Delete scribble you drew

On toolbar, click (eraser). Click scribble object to delete it.

9 Add note flag to call attention to heading

Click again to quit erasing. Click anywhere in **Babbage** subhead.

In **Note Flags** pane of **Formatting Palette**, click arrow at right of (note flag), and choose one you like.

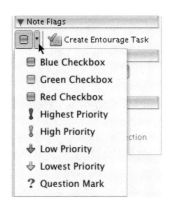

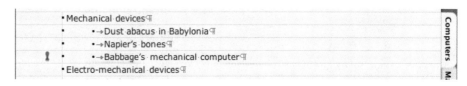

10 Find text in document

Click **Math** tab at right. Click toolbar's **Quick Search** text box, then type compu and tap RETURN.

Tab of section containing search text is highlighted in blue.

Click blue **Computers** tab. Notice that found text on page is highlighted.

11 Change view to normal, then back to notebook layout

In normal view, section tabs appear as section breaks. You'll learn more about section breaks on page 61.

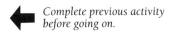
Explore recording

Using notebook layout, you can synchronize your notes with a live recording of a lecture or concert.

---

1 **Look at audio notes toolbar**

On toolbar, click 🎤 (audio notes toolbar). Put pointer on each tool in new toolbar, and read description.

Bars and buttons are similar to those you'd find in applications for recording and playing sounds, such as iTunes.

2 **Prepare for annotating lecture**

Click **English** tab at right of document.

Click **Title** in box at top. Type `Lecture on "Hamlet"`.

Click in clear area of document.

3 **Start recording**

Microphone should be connected to (or built into) computer. If not, do steps anyway to see how recording works.

On new toolbar, click ⦿ (start recording).

4 **Make notes during recording**

Enter notes as they come to mind during lecture, adding subheadings as necessary.

For this activity, you can just make up any notes you like.

5 **Stop recording**

On new toolbar, click ■ (stop).

6 **Play back recording and notes**

On new toolbar, click ▷ (play). Listen to lecture, and watch notes appear in sync with recording.

During playback, you can click ❚❚ (pause) and add notes you didn't have time to enter during lecture.

7 **Delete audio when notes are complete**

Stop playback if necessary.

On **Tools** menu, choose **Audio Notes**, then **Delete Audio from Document**.

8 **Save document in your My Files folder; name it Notebook**

9 **Quit Microsoft Word**

Quitting application closes open files.

Tip

Unless the audio portion of the file is important to you (say a musical performance you're annotating), you should delete it. The audio part takes up vastly more disk space than the text part.

Insert page breaks

Microsoft Word automatically starts a new page when necessary. You can also add manual page breaks.

1 Create two-page document for use here and later

Start Microsoft Word. Open **Computers** from your **My Files** folder.

If necessary, on **View** menu, choose **Normal**.

You will copy and paste existing text several times.

Select text from top down through blank line before your name.

On **Edit** menu, choose **Copy** (or tap ⌘ C).

On **File** menu, choose **Close** to put away **Computers** document.

On standard toolbar, click 🗋 (new blank document).

On **Edit** menu, choose **Paste** (or tap ⌘ V). Repeat five or six times.

Text copied to clipboard is pasted each time.

2 Save new document in your My Files folder

On **File** menu, choose **Save**. Save with name **Twopages** in usual location.

3 View automatic page break

Using scroll bar, move through document until you see dotted line across page.

Dotted line shows where new page will begin when document is printed.

4 Select location for manual page break

Click to put insertion point anywhere in text a few lines above dotted line.

5 Insert page break (method 1)

On **Insert** menu, choose **Break**, then **Page Break** on submenu.

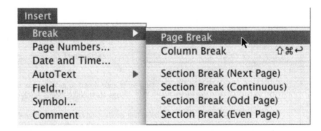

Manual break appears as dense dotted line with words "Page Break." Notice that automatic page break has disappeared.

6 Remove page break

Click to left of page break line to select it. Tap DELETE.

7 Insert page break (method 2)

Tap SHIFT ENTER. Do *not* use RETURN.

ENTER is at lower right of keyboard.

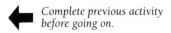

Preview document

It is always a good idea to preview a document to see page breaks before printing.

1 Preview both pages of document

On **File** menu, choose **Print Preview** (or click 🔍 on standard toolbar).

Preview toolbar replaces standard. Page appears at reduced scale.

On toolbar, click ⊞ (multiple pages).

On pop-up menu, click middle icon in first row to see two side-by-side pages (see figure at left).

2 Zoom in (method 1)

Position pointer over page you want to view more closely.

If pointer has arrow shape, click mouse button to select page.

Pointer changes shape to 🔍 *(magnifying glass with +).*

Click magnifying-glass pointer at area you want to zoom in on.

View scale is 100%, and area that you clicked appears.

3 Zoom out (method 1)

Position pointer over enlarged page.

Pointer now has minus sign: 🔍 *.*

Click page to zoom out.

Notice view scale percentage on toolbar.

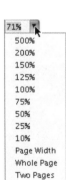

4 Zoom in (method 2)

To right of view scale, click ▾ to see zoom options.

Click **100%**.

View percentage increases. Only one page may appear.

5 Zoom out (method 2)

Display zoom pop-up menu again. Click **Two Pages**.

View percentage decreases. Two pages appear again.

6 Restore normal zoom setting of preview

On zoom menu, choose **Whole Page**.

7 Explore other buttons on toolbar

Notice 🖶 (print) on preview toolbar.

You could print document now. Instead, you'll exit preview.

8 Exit preview

Click Close on preview toolbar to return to normal view.

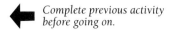

Complete previous activity before going on.

Change page margins

You can set all four margins on the page. Paragraph indents automatically adjust to the new margins.

---

1 **View margin controls**

On **Format** menu, choose **Document**. If necessary, click **Margins** in bar at top to bring that page of dialog box into view.

Top four numbers at left are sizes of page margins now.

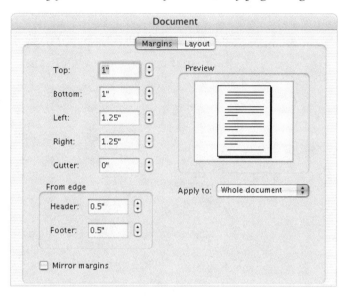

2 **Change margins, and see results**

Change left margin to **3**" and right margin to **1**". Click **OK**.

On **Formatting Palette**, click **Document** bar. Notice same margin boxes and settings as in dialog box. Close **Document** pane.

On **File** menu, choose **Print Preview** (or click 🔍) to see effect.

Click Close on preview toolbar when you're ready to go on.

3 **Mirror even and odd pages**

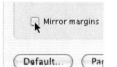

On **Format** menu, choose **Document**. Watch **Left** and **Right** labels and **Preview** area as you click **Mirror margins** check box at lower left.

Labels change to Inside *and* Outside. *Mirror margins are used for documents that will be printed on both sides of paper and need extra inside space for binding or punching holes.*

4 **Look at other options**

Notice options in **From edge** area of dialog box.

Numbers here control distance of headers and footers from top and bottom of paper. (You'll learn about headers and footers on page 59.)

Notice **Apply to** pop-up menu.

Margin changes can apply to whole document or just to parts.

5 **Cancel dialog box, and close document without saving changes**

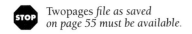 Twopages *file as saved on page 55 must be available.*

Add columns & breaks

Microsoft Word allows you to put more than one column of text on each page. You can also adjust where columns break.

1 **Open Twopages document from your My Files folder**

2 **Create two-column layout for whole document**

Change view to **Page Layout**.

View shows text within page margins.

On standard toolbar, choose **Whole Page** on zoom pop-up menu.

On **Format** menu, choose **Columns**.

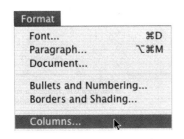

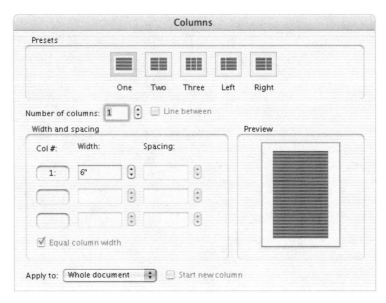

In **Presets** area, click icon labeled **Three**. Look at **Preview** area.

Click **OK**, and notice effect.

3 **Insert column break**

Click anywhere in text in column 1 of document.

On **Insert** menu, choose **Break**, then click **Column Break**.

Text after break begins in next column.

4 **Return to normal view**

On **View** menu, choose **Normal**. Scroll through text.

In normal view, text in columns appears in single narrow column.

On **Format** menu, choose **Columns**.

Under **Presets**, click icon labeled **One**; click **OK**.

Text widens to margins. Column break now serves as page break.

5 **Close document without saving changes**

Add headers & footers

*A header or footer can be used to put titles and page numbers
at the top or bottom of each page.*

1 *Open Twopages document from your My Files folder*

2 *View document with margins*

On **View** menu, choose **Page Layout**.

> *View showing margins allows you to create headers and footers.*

On zoom pop-up menu (on standard toolbar), choose **100%**.

3 *Activate header and footer areas*

> **Tip**
>
> *You can also use the* Header and
> Footer *command on the* View
> *menu. If you're in normal view, it
> automatically switches to page
> layout view, opens the header and
> footer toolbar, and activates the
> header and footer areas.*

Put pointer in top margin of page. Double click when pointer shape
changes to: 🖹 . (If shape doesn't change, use tip at left.)

> *Document text is dimmed. Dashed outline shows header area.*

On new toolbar that appears, move pointer to each icon, and read its
description. *Don't click tools yet!*

4 *Enter header text*

Notice insertion point in header area of page.

Look at tab stops in ruler.

> *Ruler shows center tab stop at 3" and right tab stop at 6".*

Tap TAB twice to move insertion point to right tab stop at 6".

Type Computer History Society.

5 *Move to footer, and enter text*

On new toolbar, click 🖺 (switch between header and footer).

> *Command jumps to footer area. Ruler settings are same as for header.*

Tap TAB to move insertion point to center tab stop at 3".

On same toolbar, click # (insert page number).

> *You should see 1 in middle of the footer area.*

Tap TAB to move to right tab stop at 6".

On same toolbar, click 🗓 (insert date).

> *Current date is inserted. (Date is updated when you open or print
> document.)*

6 *View two pages*

On zoom pop-up menu, choose **Two Pages**.

Drag lower-right corner of window to make it as wide as possible.

Notice that header and footer items are same on both pages.

7   **Switch between body text and header and footer text**

Double-click anywhere in body text of document.

Toolbar disappears. Header and footer text is dimmed. Body text is active.

Double-click in any header or footer text.

Toolbar returns. Now you can edit headers and footers.

8   **Edit headers**

Triple-click any text in header on page 1. Notice that same text is selected on page 2.

On **Font** pane of **Formatting Palette**, click **B** (bold).

Both headers are now bold.

By the way

You can also have different headers and footers on left and right pages if the document is to be printed on both sides of the paper. On the Format *menu, choose* Documents. *On the* Layout *page of the dialog box, click* Different odd and even.

9   **Make headers and footers different on first page**

On headers-and-footers toolbar, click 1 (different first page).

Header and footer no longer appear on first page. Also, dashed boxes there say First Page Header *and* First Page Footer.

10 **Add special header on page 1**

Click anywhere in **First Page Header** box.

With insertion point in header area, tap TAB, and type CHS .

First page now has header, but it's different from all others.

11 **Restore normal view**

Drag lower-right corner of window to make it normal width.

On zoom pop-up menu, choose **Page Width**.

On **View** menu, choose **Normal**.

Headers and footers are hidden in this view.

12 **Close document without saving changes**

STOP Twopages *file as saved on page 55 must be available.*

Create sections

Sections are like book chapters. Each section can have different headers and page margins and a different column layout.

1 **Open Twopages document from your My Files folder**

If necessary, choose **Normal** on **View** menu.

```
Page Break
Column Break                ⇧⌘↵

Section Break (Next Page)
Section Break (Continuous)
Section Break (Odd Page)
Section Break (Even Page)
```

2 **Add section break**

Put insertion point just before first word in text paragraph 4 (Today).

On **Insert** menu, put pointer on **Break**. Look at four **Section Break** options on submenu.

All but Continuous *will cause next section to begin new page.*

Choose **Section Break (Continuous)**.

Nonprinting section break character is inserted. Symbol for character is double row of dotted lines with Section Break (Continuous) *in middle.*

Change to **Page Layout** view. Change zoom percentage to **Two Pages**.

Because you chose Continuous, *no page break occurs at new section.*

3 **Change format of section 2**

By the way
The format change affects just the section with the insertion point (or any selected text).

If necessary, click anywhere below **Section Break (Continuous)** marker.

On **Format** menu, choose **Columns**.

Under **Presets**, click icon labeled **Two**. Click **OK**.

First three paragraphs are in single column. Rest are in two columns.

4 **Change type of section break**

With insertion point still in section 2, choose **Document** from **Format** menu.

In bar near top of dialog box, click **Layout**.

On **Section start** pop-up menu, choose **New page**. Click **OK**.

Section 2 now starts new page.

5 **Delete section break, and see result**

Click anywhere inside **Section Break (Next Page)** marker.

Tap [SHIFT]→ to select marker.

Marker isn't highlighted, but it is selected. You delete selection as usual.

By the way
Whenever you remove a column break, a page break, or even a paragraph mark from text, the part before the break takes on the formats of the part after the break.

Tap [DELETE].

Old section 1 takes on two-column format of section 2

6 **Restore view**

On zoom pop-up menu, choose **Page Width**.

On **View** menu, choose **Normal**.

7 **Close document without saving changes**

STOP Computers *file as saved on page 19 must be available.*

Insert table

You can easily add tabular information to a Microsoft Word document without setting tab stops.

1 Open Computers document from your My Files folder

You'll insert table just below text paragraph 1.

2 Prepare to insert

Click just before paragraph mark at end of text paragraph 1. Tap (RETURN) twice.

Insertion point should be on blank line. You'll insert table here. It's always good to leave blank space around table.

3 Insert table

On **Table** menu, choose **Insert**, then **Table**.

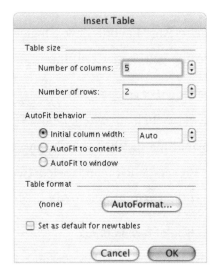

Type 4 for **Number of columns**; tap (TAB); type 4 for **Number of rows**. Click **OK**.

Empty table with four columns and four rows appears in document. Rectangles formed by intersections of rows and columns are called "cells."

4 Enter data in table

Insertion point should already be in first cell.

Type **Computers in Use**. Tap (TAB) to move to next cell.

Type **1990** (TAB) **1995** (TAB) **2000**.

Tap (TAB) to move to next cell.

Insertion point moves to next row.

Continue entering text to create table shown below. Do *not* tap (TAB) after last entry.

By the way

The numbers used in this example are simply figures for the exercise and bear no relation to the actual numbers (which are much larger).

Computers in Use	1990	1995	2000	
Business	50,000	70,000	98,000	
School	20,000	35,000	87,000	
Home	10,000	25,000	60,000	

5 **Save document with new name**

On **File** menu, choose **Save As**.

Save with name `Table` in your usual location.

6 **Select rows and columns**

Put arrow pointer just left of row 2. Click to select whole row.

Put pointer just above column 3.

Watch pointer change to ↓ .

Click to select column.

With OPTION held down, click anywhere in column 2 to select it.

With OPTION held down, double-click anywhere in table to select all cells.

7 **Format table**

Select row 1.

In **Font** pane of **Formatting Palette**, click **B** (bold) to add bold style to labels.

Select column 1.

In **Font** pane of **Formatting Palette**, click **B** *twice* to make labels bold.

8 **Adjust column width**

Select all cells in table.

With SHIFT held down, on ruler, put pointer over first column divider (at 1.5").

> *Pressing* SHIFT *allows you to move one column divider at a time.*

Watch pointer change to ▯. Press and drag left to 1" mark.

> *Width of column 1 is reduced.*

Use above steps to adjust other column widths to 1 inch also.

9 **Select columns 2, 3, and 4**

Position pointer at top of column 2.

Watch pointer change to ↓ .

Press and drag to right, being careful to keep pointer in table.

10 **Change text alignment in selected cells**

On **Formatting Palette**, in **Alignment and Spacing** pane, click ≣ (align center).

> *Text is centered within cells in all three columns.*

By the way

You must click bold twice to format column 1 because bold was applied to the first cell when you added bold to row 1. The first click removes bold from the first cell in the column; the second click applies bold to the entire column.

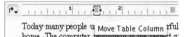

Today many people u Move Table Column rful
home. The computer revolution is the fastest-g

11 *Center table on page*

Select all cells in table. On **Table** menu, choose **Table Properties**.

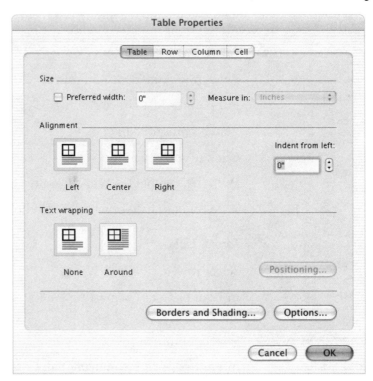

In **Alignment** area, click **Center**, then click **OK**.

Table is centered horizontally on page.

12 *Add shading*

Select all cells in row 1.

On **Formatting Palette**, click **Borders and Shading** bar.

In **Shading** area, on **Pattern** pop-up menu, choose **20%**.

Close **Borders and Shading** pane of palette.

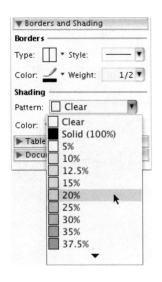

13 *Click outside table to see formatting*

Computers in Use¤	1990¤	1995¤	2000¤	¤
Business¤	50,000¤	70,000¤	98,000¤	¤
School¤	20,000¤	35,000¤	87,000¤	¤
Home¤	10,000¤	25,000¤	60,000¤	¤

14 *Save changed document*

15 *Quit Word*

If you're using floppy disk and not continuing now, eject disk as shown on page 5, step 5.

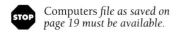
Set up mail merge

You can create a form letter and a data document with names and addresses. Then you can merge the two.

1 Create new document for name and address data

Start Word if necessary. If Word is already running, on standard toolbar, click 🗋 (new blank document).

Data document for merge is ordinary word processing document with table containing data you want used. First step is to insert blank table.

2 Insert table to hold data

On **Table** menu, choose **Insert**, then **Table**.

Type 6 for **Number of columns**; tap TAB; type 4 for **Number of rows**.

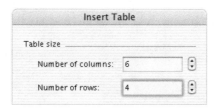

Click **OK**.

Six columns will hold first name, last name, address, city, state, zip code.

3 Enter headings in first row

Insertion point should already be in first cell.

Type following text:

First TAB Last TAB Street TAB City TAB State TAB Zip

Column headings are names of data fields. You'll use these field names in your form letter instead of any actual data for a person.

4 Enter name and address data

Tap TAB to go to first cell in next row.

Enter data shown in figure below, tapping TAB between entries. Substitute your own name and address in first row. Do *not* tap TAB after last entry.

Don't worry if text wraps to next line. It won't affect mail merge.

First¤	Last¤	Street¤	City¤	State¤	Zip¤	⌐
Bonita¤	Sebastian¤	123 Maple St.¤	Santa Cruz¤	CA¤	95060¤	⌐
Valerie¤	Whitman¤	345 Main St.¤	Garden City¤	IA¤	50101¤	⌐
Bill¤	Gates¤	789 Hunt St.¤	Redmond¤	WA¤	98052¤	⌐

5 Save and close data document

If using floppy disk, insert it now. Wait for drive activity to stop.

On **File** menu, choose **Save**. Save with name **People** in your usual location.

On **File** menu, choose **Close**.

6 **Open, rename, and save document to become form**

Open **Computers** document from your **My Files** folder.

Form letter document will be based on this document.

On **File** menu, choose **Save As**.

Save with name **Formltr** in your usual location.

7 **Convert document to form for merge**

On **Tools** menu, choose **Data Merge Manager**.

You'll use this palette to create form (main document), link it to data document, and merge both to create finished document.

In **Main Document** pane, click **Create** to see pop-up menu.

On **Create** pop-up menu, choose **Form Letters**.

Data Merge Manager shows items you selected.

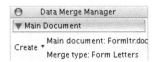

Formltr is now set as main document for merge. (To convert file back to normal Word document, you would use last option on Create pop-up menu.)

8 **Link form document to data document**

In **Data Source** pane of **Data Merge Manager**, click **Get Data**.

On **Get Data** pop-up menu, choose **Open Data Source**.

Navigate to your **My Files** folder, and open **People** document.

Data Merge Manager shows People is now set as data source for merge.

Tip

You can use the same data document to print mailing labels or envelopes. Start at the Create pop-up menu on the Data Merge Manager. Then choose Labels or Envelopes, and follow the steps to create the document.

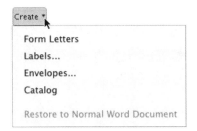

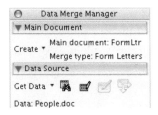

9 **Add extra lines at top of document for merge fields**

Make sure insertion point is at beginning of **Formltr** document.

Tap RETURN twice to add two blank lines.

Tap ⌘ HOME (FN ⌘ HOME on laptop) to return to top of document.

10 **Insert fields from People data document into Formltr form document**

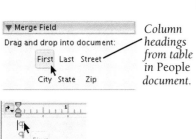

Column headings from table in People document.

In **Merge Field** pane of **Data Merge Manager**, notice merge field names.

If field names do not appear, click ▼ *in* Merge Field *pane or check selected data document.*

Put pointer over **First** field name. Notice outline.

Press and drag to move **First** to beginning of document.

«First» *is inserted into form document at insertion point. Angle brackets mark it as merge field.*

11 **Insert another field on same line of text**

Tap spacebar to insert space character.

Press and drag to move **Last** to insertion point.

«Last» *is inserted after space you typed.*

12 **Insert more fields**

Tap RETURN to insert new line. Drag **Street** to insertion point.

Tap RETURN. Drag **City** to insertion point.

Type , (comma) and one space. Drag **State** to insertion point.

Tap spacebar twice. Drag **Zip** to insertion point.

Tap RETURN twice to insert two blank lines.

Type Dear and one space. Drag **First** to insertion point.

Type , (comma).

Beginning of document should look like figure below. Fields are for inside address and salutation of letters.

«First» «Last» ¶
«Street» ¶
«City», «State» «Zip» ¶
¶
Dear «First», ¶

13 **Save Formltr document in your usual location**

You now have People *document with data and* Formltr *document with field names and text. Next step is to merge data into form.*

← *Complete previous activity before going on.*

Do mail merge

Once you've created a main document, linked it to a data document, and inserted placeholders, you're ready to merge.

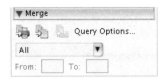

1 *Preview merge*

Click **Preview** in **Data Merge Manager** to see pane with options.

Click 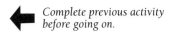 (view merged data).

> *Your name and address appear at top of* Formltr *document.*

Use arrow buttons under **Preview** to view letters to others.

Click {a} (view field codes).

> *Data are gone, and codes reappear.*

Click {a} again, then (view merged data) to turn off.

2 *Create merged document*

In **Merge** pane of **Data Merge Manager**, click (merge to new document).

> *Single merged document named* Form Letters1 *is created; errors, if any, appear. (If there are errors, take care of them, and perform merge again.)*

Tip

Options in the Merge pane allow you to merge directly to a printer or e-mail or to print only some records.

---

3 *Review letters*

Scroll through new **Form Letters1** document, and look at inside addresses.

> *Letters are separated by section breaks (ones that also start new pages).*

4 *Preview merged letters*

On **File** menu, choose **Print Preview**.

Use (multiple pages) to see all pages. Zoom in to see inside address on each page.

Click Close when finished.

5 *Save merged document*

On **File** menu, choose **Save**.

Save file with name **Merge** in your usual location.

6 *Close Data Merge Manager palette*

7 *Print merged letters (optional)*

On **File** menu, choose **Print**. Set options you want; then click **OK**.

8 *Close all documents*

Press and hold (SHIFT) down. On **File** menu, choose **Close All**.

If asked, save changes.

9 *Quit Microsoft Word; if using floppy disk, eject it as usual*

Insert hyperlink

You can create a link in one document that, when clicked, takes the user to another document.

1 **Start Microsoft Word; open Computers document from your My Files folder**

2 **Insert Hyperlink to CHSNote document**

In first paragraph of **Computers** document, select **fastest-growing technology**.

By the way

You can also create a hyperlink from a Word document on your computer to a page on the World Wide Web. If you don't know the page name, or URL, you can browse the Web and find it.

On **Insert** menu, choose **Hyperlink** (or tap ⌘ K). In bar near top of dialog box, click **Document**. Click **Select** button.

In **Choose a File** dialog box, navigate to your **My Files** folder (location where your files are stored). Double-click **CHSNote** document in list.

Document name (possibly preceded by other text) appears in Link to *box.*

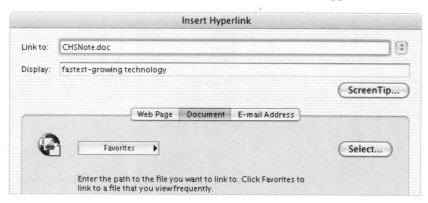

Click **OK**. Notice underline and color of hyperlink text.

3 **Use link to open document**

By the way

If your files are saved in a folder on a network disk, the box above the pointer will have additional text before the file name. The code %20 stands for the space character.

Position pointer over hyperlink. Notice pointer shape and box above it.

Click hyperlink.

CHSNote document opens and becomes active. Web toolbar appears.

Look at file list on **Window** menu.

Both Computers *and* CHSNote *are now open.*

4 **Move back and forth between documents**

On new Web toolbar, click ← (back) to see **Computers** document.

On new Web toolbar, click → (forward) to see **CHSNote** document.

Buttons work like same buttons on Web browser.

5 **Quit Microsoft Word without saving changes**

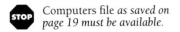
Save as Web page

You can convert an existing document to a Web page document. Word creates the hypertext markup language (HTML) code.

1 **Start Microsoft Word; open Computers document from your My Files folder**

2 **Change Computers document**

Delete all text except paragraphs shown in figure below.

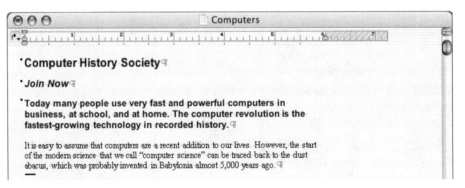

Put insertion point at start of first paragraph.

Type `Computer History Society` [RETURN].

Type `Join Now` [RETURN].

Click anywhere in first new line.

In **Styles** pane of **Formatting Palette**, on **Pick style to apply** list, choose **Heading 1**.

Click anywhere in second new line. Change style to **Heading 2**.

Click in first body paragraph. Change style to **Heading 3**.

> *Text should now look like figure below.*

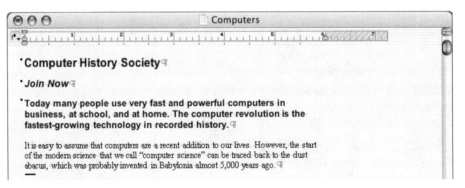

3 **Rename and save document as Web page**

On **File** menu, choose **Save as Web Page** (*not* Save).

Type `CHSWeb.htm` as file name.

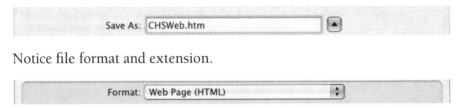

Notice file format and extension.

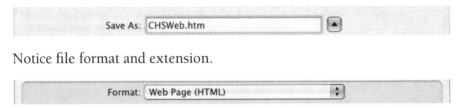

> *Web browsers look for .htm extension.*

Navigate to your usual location for saving files.

Click **Save**.

4 *Quit Word, and check document type of new file*

On **Word** menu, choose **Quit Word**. Close all open windows.

On desktop, double-click **Macintosh HD**. In left pane, click **My Disk** or **Documents**. In right pane, double-click your **My Files** folder.

On **View** menu, choose **as Icons**.

Scroll as necessary to see **CHSWeb.htm** icon.

> *Icon is for file you just saved. It is different from Word file icons.*

Click **CHSWeb.htm** icon. On **File** menu, choose **Get Info**.

> *Top of dialog box shows kind of file. (Yours may be different.)*

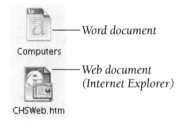

—*Word document*

Computers

—*Web document (Internet Explorer)*

CHSWeb.htm

By the way

The icon shapes you see may vary from the ones in these figures.

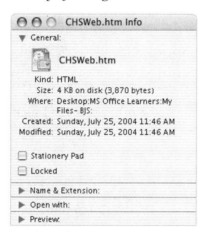

Click 🔴⊖○ to close **CHSWeb.htm info** window.

5 *Open file in Web browser*

Double-click **CHSWeb.htm** icon.

> *Your Web browser program (usually Internet Explorer) begins running and opens file CHSWeb. Contents and format are same as in original Word file.*

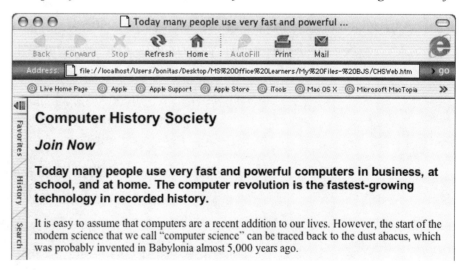

6 **View HTML (hypertext markup language) codes in document**

On **View** menu, choose **Source**. Widen window if necessary to see all text.

Text between angle brackets is HTML format code.

Scroll down until you see   `<h1>Computer History Society</h1>` .

This part of document has text (with format codes) for Web page.

Actual text in file ———
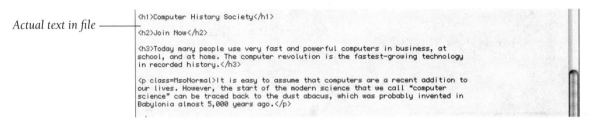

```
<h1>Computer History Society</h1>

<h2>Join Now</h2>

<h3>Today many people use very fast and powerful computers in business, at
school, and at home. The computer revolution is the fastest-growing technology
in recorded history.</h3>

<p class=MsoNormal>It is easy to assume that computers are a recent addition to
our lives. However, the start of the modern science that we call "computer
science" can be traced back to the dust abacus, which was probably invented in
Babylonia almost 5,000 years ago.</p>
```

Browser program interprets codes and formats text accordingly.

7 **Quit browser program, and reopen Web document in Microsoft Word**

On **Explorer** (or other browser) menu, choose **Quit**. Close any windows you see.

Restart Microsoft Word. On **File** menu, choose **Open**.

Navigate to your folder where you save files (see page 21).

CHSWeb.htm is "grayed out" in list of files.

At top of dialog box, look at **Enable** setting.

Enable: All Office Documents

All Office Documents means Word, Excel, and PowerPoint documents.

Use pop-up menu to enable **All Readable Documents**.

CHSWeb.htm icon is no longer "grayed out."

Use **Enable** pop-up menu to change type to **Web Pages**.

Now other file icons are "grayed out."

Double-click **CHSWeb.htm** in list area.

Document opens in Word, in online layout view. You could use this view or switch to normal for more editing or formatting if you wish. Appearance is same as in Web browser.

8 **Quit Microsoft Word, and shut down computer**

On **Word** menu, choose **Quit Word**. Don't save changes if asked.

If you're using floppy disk, eject it as shown on page 5, step 5.

On Apple menu, choose **Shut Down**.

Start Microsoft PowerPoint

To learn the graphics tools available in Microsoft Office 2004, you'll use the Microsoft PowerPoint application.

1 **Start computer and PowerPoint**

Switch on computer (see page 2). Do all steps on page 7, but choosing **Microsoft PowerPoint** (see icon at left).

Display should look similar to figure below.

Menu bar

Standard toolbar

Title bar

Slide you'll draw objects on

View scale (yours may be different)

View buttons

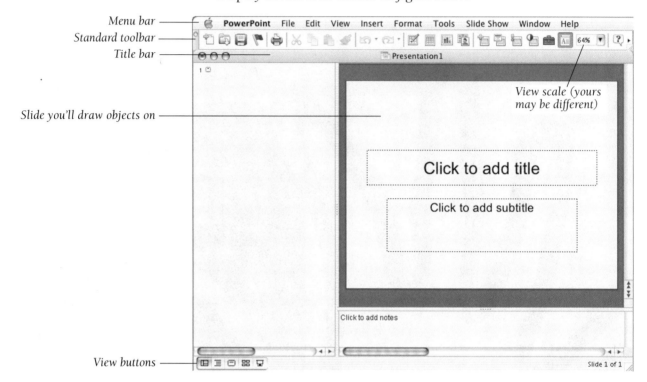

2 **Change to blank layout**

On **Formatting Palette**, make sure **Change Slides** pane is in view.

Near top of pane, click 📇 (slide layout).

Selected layout at upper left is for "title slide" now in window.

At bottom of pane, click ▬▾ to see more possible layouts.

Put pointer on blank layout at lower right.

You'll use blank slide now for learning to use Office 2004 drawing tools.

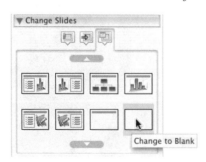

By the way

A slide in PowerPoint is like a page in a word processing document.

Click selected layout in figure above.

Complete previous activity before going on.

Set preferences

User settings can affect the way PowerPoint looks and works.
You'll set view options and preferences as expected in this book.

1 **Set view options**

On menu bar, click **View**. Click as necessary so check marks appear only for **Slide** and **Ruler**.

With **View** menu down, put pointer on **Toolbars**. Click as necessary so check marks appear only for **Standard** and **Drawing**.

2 **Set preferences**

On **PowerPoint** menu, choose **Preferences**. Click names in bar at top to see different pages. Make options match figures below.

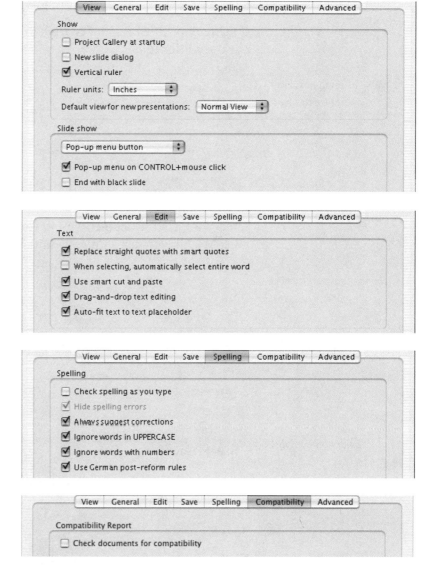

Click **OK** to approve all settings.

3 **Disable AutoCorrect settings**

On **Tools** menu, choose **AutoCorrect**. Remove any check marks you see. Click **OK**.

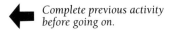
Save file

After creating a new document, you should name it and save it.
As you add to the document, you can easily save changes.

1 **Give Save command**

If using floppy disk, make sure it's in drive now.

On **File** menu, choose **Save** (or click 🖬 on standard toolbar).

2 **Name presentation file**

In **Save As** box, type Drawing as name of file. Leave any extension.

3 **Navigate to location where you will save file**

If three panes in figure below do not appear on sheet, click 🔽 at right of **Save As** text box, to see paths to locations.

If using floppy disk, click **My Disk** in top part of left pane. In middle pane, click **My Files** folder with your initials.

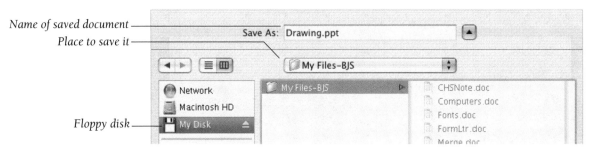

Otherwise, click **Documents** in lower part of left pane. In middle pane, click **My Files** folder with your initials.

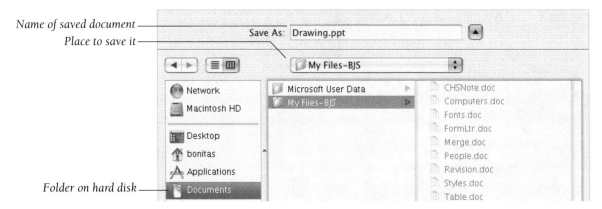

If necessary, click **Append file extension** check box to add **.ppt** to document name.

4 **Save file**

Click **Save** to save document with name **Drawing**.

> *Title bar now shows new file name. In future, when you give Save command for this file, no dialog box will appear; changed file replaces original.*

Complete previous activity before going on.

Draw graphic objects

Microsoft Office provides tools to help you draw simple or complex objects. You'll use PowerPoint to explore the tools.

1 **Look at drawing tools**

Locate drawing toolbar (normally vertical at left of window). If not present, on **View** menu, choose **Toolbars**, then **Drawing**).

Move pointer along toolbar. For each tool, read name below pointer.

2 **Draw simple object (method 1)**

On drawing toolbar, click □ (rectangle).

Button highlight shows which tool is active.

Position pointer near upper-left corner of slide area.

Pointer shape is now crosshair.

Press mouse button, and drag down and to right.

Release mouse button.

Colored rectangle with black outline appears where you drew. Active tool now is ▣ (select objects) at top of drawing toolbar. Pointer shape is arrow.

3 **Draw simple object (method 2)**

On drawing toolbar, click □ (rectangle). Click in blank area to right of object you just drew.

Small equal-sided rectangle (square) appears where you clicked. Rectangle tool is no longer active.

4 **Deselect and select object**

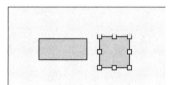

Notice handles (tiny white squares) on border of square object.

Handles mean object is selected. Many commands affect only selected objects.

Click arrow pointer in clear area of slide to deselect object.

Put pointer inside rectangle. Notice that pointer shape changes to hand.

Click pointer inside rectangle. Notice handles.

Rectangle is now selected.

5 **Save changed file**

If you're using floppy disk, make sure it's still in drive.

On **File** menu, choose **Save** (or click 🖫 on standard toolbar).

No Save As dialog sheet slides down this time. File is saved in your My Files folder, replacing original Drawing file.

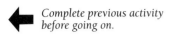
Move, resize & delete object

After you have created an object, you may wish to modify it by moving it, changing its size or shape, or deleting it.

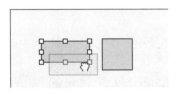

By the way

You can switch the invisible snapping grid off. Click the top button on the drawing toolbar, and move the pointer to Snap at the bottom. If To Grid is checked on the submenu, the snapping grid is in effect. Click To Grid to disable it.

1 **Move object (method 1)**

Put pointer inside rectangle. Notice that pointer becomes hand.

Press mouse button, and drag to right and down as in figure at left.

Release mouse button.

> *Rectangle moves to new location. It may snap to invisible grid that helps align objects. See By the Way at left.*

2 **Move object (method 2)**

Click inside square to select object.

Watch object as you tap each arrow key on keyboard three or four times.

> *Selected object moves in small increments in direction of arrow.*

3 **Make object smaller**

Click inside rectangle to select object.

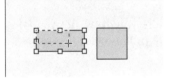

Move pointer carefully to handle at lower right. Notice change in pointer shape: 🔳 .

Press mouse button, and drag handle up and to left, as in figure at left.

Notice change in pointer shape as you drag.

Release mouse button.

> *Rectangle is smaller.*

4 **Make object larger**

Follow step 3, except drag handle down and to right. Notice change in pointer shape as you drag.

Release mouse button.

> *Rectangle is larger.*

5 **Change width of object**

Click inside square to select object.

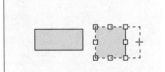

Move pointer carefully to handle at middle of right side. Notice change in pointer shape: 🔳 .

Press mouse button, and drag handle to right, as in figure at left.

Release mouse button.

> *Square is widened into rectangle.*

6 **Delete both objects**

Click inside rectangle on left to select it. Tap DELETE.

Use same method to select and delete other object.

! *A PowerPoint file must be open in slide view.*

Use drawing aids

Freehand drawing can be difficult. Microsoft PowerPoint has aids that ease the task.

1 Draw equal-sided object

On drawing toolbar, click ☐ (rectangle).

On keyboard, hold (SHIFT) down.

Position pointer near upper-left corner of slide area.

Press mouse button, and drag down and to right.

Release mouse button first, then (SHIFT).

> *Equal-sided rectangle (square) appears.*

Tip

You can also create a standard-size equal-sided object by clicking with a tool in a blank area. Pressing and dragging lets you control the size of the object.

2 Move object horizontally or vertically

If object has no handles, click inside object to select it.

With (SHIFT) down, try to move object diagonally to right and down.

> *You can move object only horizontally or vertically while pressing (SHIFT).*

Release mouse button first, then (SHIFT).

3 Resize object without changing shape

Make sure object has handles.

On keyboard, hold (SHIFT) down.

Move pointer over handle at lower right.

Press and drag diagonally to right and down.

Release mouse button, then (SHIFT).

> *Square is enlarged but keeps shape. Other objects also keep shapes when resized with (SHIFT) down.*

4 Delete object

Make sure object has handles. Tap (DELETE).

5 Draw object from center out

On drawing toolbar, click ☐ again.

On keyboard, press and hold (OPTION).

Position pointer near middle of slide area.

Press mouse button, and drag down and to right.

> *Object grows in all directions from place where you began to drag.*

Release mouse button first, then (OPTION).

6 Delete object

Make sure object has handles. Tap (DELETE).

Use drawing aids *continued*

7 *Draw equal-sided object from center out*

On drawing toolbar, click ☐ again.

On keyboard, hold both (OPTION) and (SHIFT) down.

From middle of slide area, press and drag down and to right. Release mouse button, then keys.

> *Square is drawn from center out. Same method works with other objects.*

8 *Use guides*

On **View** menu, choose **Guides** (or tap ⌘ G).

> *Dotted horizontal and vertical guides appear.*

Put pointer on vertical guide outside square. Press and drag to right.

Drag horizontal guide up slightly.

> *Notice that distance (in inches from center) appears at pointer.*

Watch square as you drag it near either guide.

> *Edge or center of square "jumps" to guide.*

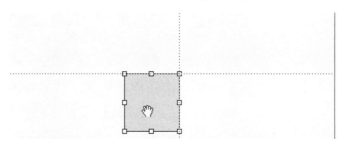

Delete square.

9 *Use guides to position new object*

On drawing toolbar, click ☐ again.

On keyboard, press and hold (SHIFT)(OPTION).

Position pointer at intersection of guides.

Press mouse button, and drag diagonally. Release mouse button, then keys.

> *Result is square with center exactly at place guides cross.*

Delete object.

10 *Switch guides off*

On **View** menu, choose **Guides** (or tap ⌘ G)again.

11 *Close file without saving changes*

STOP Drawing *file as saved on page 77 must be available.*

Select objects

Many commands act only on selected objects. You can select one object or several objects at once.

1 **Open Drawing file**

If you're using floppy disk, make sure it's in drive now.

On **File** menu, choose **Open** (or click 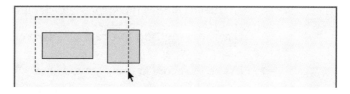 on standard toolbar).

Use navigation method on page 19, step 3, as needed to reach location with your saved files. Then double-click **Drawing** in list.

2 **Select single object on slide**

Click pointer inside rectangle. Click square. Click clear area of slide.

Handles appear when object is selected.

3 **Use selection marquee to select several objects**

In slide area, position pointer above and to left of rectangle.

Press and drag diagonally so "marquee" (dashed outline) is like figure.

Release mouse button.

Square is not selected. Only objects completely inside selection marquee are selected.

By the way

Selection handles on shapes other than rectangles appear on an invisible bounding rectangle.

---

4 **Add object to selection**

Hold (SHIFT) down as you click inside square.

5 **Remove object from selection**

Hold (SHIFT) down as you click inside rectangle.

6 **Delete selected object**

On **Edit** menu, choose **Clear** (or tap (DELETE)).

7 **Undo change**

On **Edit** menu, choose **Undo Clear** (or tap (⌘ Z) or click 🔄 on standard toolbar).

8 **Select both objects**

On **Edit** menu, choose **Select All** (or tap (⌘ A)).

9 **Deselect both selected objects**

Click in slide area away from any object.

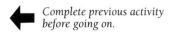
Use line tools

In addition to the rectangle tool, Microsoft PowerPoint provides many special tools for other objects.

1 *Add blank slide*

On **Insert** menu, choose **New Slide** (or click 📋 on standard toolbar).

2 *Display line tools*

On drawing toolbar, click ✏️⁻ (lines) to see menu.

Move pointer to double horizontal bar at top of menu. Read tip.

Click bar to float menu as **Lines** palette.

3 *Draw straight lines*

On **Lines** palette, double-click ＼ (line).

In slide area, press and drag diagonally to draw line, then release. Notice that line tool remains selected.

With (SHIFT) held down, draw line to right. Release mouse button, then key.

> (SHIFT) *makes line exactly horizontal.*

Use same method to draw exactly vertical and exactly diagonal lines.

4 *Use scribble tool to draw curved lines*

On **Lines** palette, click ✒️ (scribble).

In clear slide area, press and drag to begin drawing object.

> *Pointer changes from crosshair to pencil shape.*

Continue pressing and dragging to create object. Release mouse button to end drawing.

> *Object is selected. You can use same methods as before to move, resize, reshape, or delete object (see page 78).*

Tip

If you are having trouble selecting a scribble object, click on its line.

5 *Use freeform tool to draw polygons*

On **Lines** palette, click ⬠ (freeform).

Position pointer over clear area of slide. Click to establish starting point.

Move pointer to new position, and click to create first line segment.

Continue moving and clicking (*not* dragging) to draw polygon.

Click starting point to close polygon.

> *Object is filled with color and selected. You can use same methods as before to move, resize, or delete object (see page 78).*

By the way

You can double-click to end a polygon at any point without closing it. If the polygon is not closed, it will not have a fill color.

6 *Close Lines palette*

Click 🔘 (close) at left of title bar on **Lines** palette.

7 *Save changed file in your My Files folder*

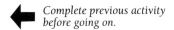
Draw basic shapes

PowerPoint has dozens of drawing tools that automatically create complex, useful objects for your slides.

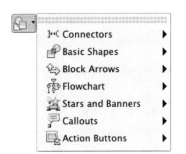

1 **Add blank slide**

On standard toolbar, click ▤ (new slide).

> *New blank slide appears. You can use ▲▼ at lower-right of window to move from one slide to another.*

2 **Display Basic Shapes palette**

On drawing toolbar, click ▣ ▾ (autoshapes).

Move pointer to **Basic Shapes**, then right and to bar at top of submenu. Click bar to float palette.

> *You can press and drag title bar to move palette where you want in window.*

3 **Use Basic Shapes drawing tools**

Click tool that looks like first object in figure below.

Click in slide area to draw object. Move and resize as needed.

Use tools on basic shapes palette to draw other objects in figure.

> *When selected, some shapes have extra diamond-shaped handle. You'll learn what this means on page 84.*

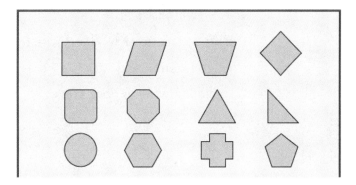

4 **Add new blank slide as in step 1**

5 **Draw large cube**

On **Basic Shapes** palette, click ▱ (cube).

Position pointer over clear area of slide.

Press and drag diagonally, making cube large.

Release mouse button.

6 **Close Basic Shapes palette**

Click ▣ (close) in title bar of **Basic Shapes** palette.

7 **Save file with two new slides**

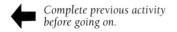
Modify objects

AutoShapes and freeform objects often have special handles for modifying their shapes.

1 **Adjust shape of AutoShape object**

Select cube. Notice yellow, diamond-shaped handle at left.

> *Many objects created using AutoShape tools have adjustment handle in addition to regular selection handles.*

Press and drag adjustment handle down. Release mouse button.

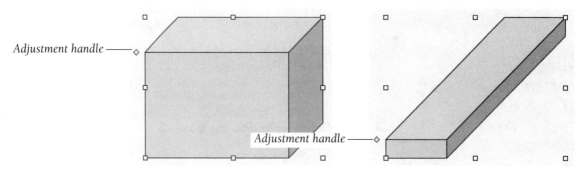

Adjustment handle

Adjustment handle

Notice that object retains same bounding handles and position.

2 **Undo change**

On **Edit** menu, choose **Undo Adjust Object** (or click 🔄 on toolbar).

3 **Edit freeform object**

Click scroll bar to view slide 2 with freeform object you drew (page 82).

Click polygon to select it.

At top of drawing toolbar, click 🔷 ▾ (draw) to see menu.

Choose **Edit Points**.

> *Tiny black square appears at each place you clicked to create object.*

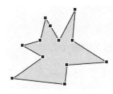

Drag tiny squares on object to change shape.

Put pointer on line between squares. Press and drag away from line.

> *New square (point) appears where button was released.*

When finished, click outside object.

4 **Return to first slide; save and close file**

Use upper arrow on ⬍ at lower right of window to go to first slide.

On **File** menu, choose **Save**.

On **File** menu, choose **Close**.

Duplicate objects

Frequently you want multiple copies of the same object. You can copy and paste objects or duplicate objects.

1 *Create new presentation with blank slide*

On **File** menu, choose **New Presentation**.

Use **Formatting Palette** to choose blank slide layout (see page 74, step 2)

On **View** menu, choose **Slide**.

2 *Copy and paste object*

Use □ (rectangle) to draw small rectangle on left side of slide.

Make sure object is selected.

On **Edit** menu, choose **Copy** (or click 📋 on standard toolbar).

On **Edit** menu, choose **Paste** (or click 📋 on standard toolbar).

Copy appears slightly below and to right of original.

Move copy to right, and line up with original.

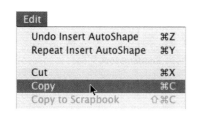

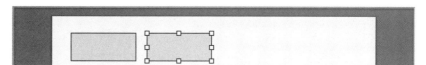

On **Edit** menu, choose **Paste** again.

Another copy appears in same place as first copy originally appeared.

3 *Select and delete both copies; leave original*

4 *Duplicate object*

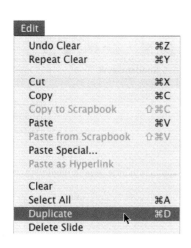

Select rectangle. On **Edit** menu, choose **Duplicate**.

So far, effect is same as copying and pasting.

Move copy to right, and line up with original, as in figure above.

On **Edit** menu, choose **Duplicate**.

This copy is pasted in relation to second as you positioned second in relation to original. Both object and its location are duplicated.

On **Edit** menu, choose **Duplicate**.

This copy is pasted in relation to third as third was pasted in relation to second.

5 *Move and resize rectangles*

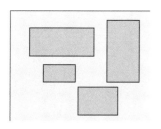

Make rectangles resemble figure at left.

Use keyboard arrow keys to nudge objects.

6 *Save new file*

On **File** menu, choose **Save**. Save file with name **Objects** in usual location.

Attach text to objects

Frequently when you create an object, you put a label on it. In Microsoft PowerPoint, you can attach the text to the object.

1   **Attach label to first rectangle**

Select large rectangle at left.

> *White selection handles indicate object is selected.*

Using uppercase letters, type your first name.

> *Name appears in middle of object. Thick border appears when selected object has text attached. Border is striped when text is being entered or edited.*

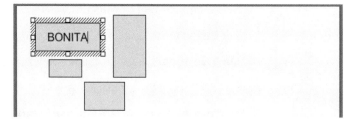

Click same rectangle away from text or in border. Drag to right.

> *Text moves with object. It is attached. Border is no longer striped because you are not editing text.*

Return rectangle to original location.

2   **Edit attached text**

Double-click your name in rectangle.

> *Text is highlighted. Striping returns to border.*

Type JOHN.

> *Entered text replaces highlighted text, as usual.*

3   **Add attached text to second rectangle**

Select tall rectangle to right, and type VAL.

4   **Add attached text to third and fourth rectangles**

Follow steps above to create figure below.

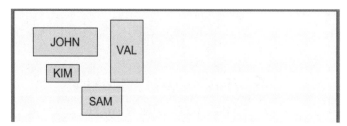

5   **Save changed Objects file**

*Complete previous activity
before going on.*

Change object fill

*New PowerPoint objects are filled with a solid pale aqua. You
can modify the fill attribute in several ways.*

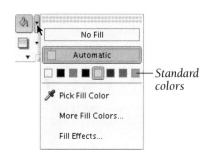
*—Standard
colors*

1 Switch object fill off and back on

Select rectangle **JOHN**.

At bottom of drawing toolbar, click arrow at right of (fill color).

On menu that appears, click **No Fill**.

> *Fill color is removed. Rectangle is transparent now. Text remains.*

On drawing toolbar, again click arrow at right of . Click **Automatic**.

> *Standard (solid pale aqua) fill is added to object.*

2 Change object fill color

Make sure rectangle **JOHN** is still selected.

On **Format** menu, choose **Colors and Lines**.

In **Fill** area, click to display **Color** menu.

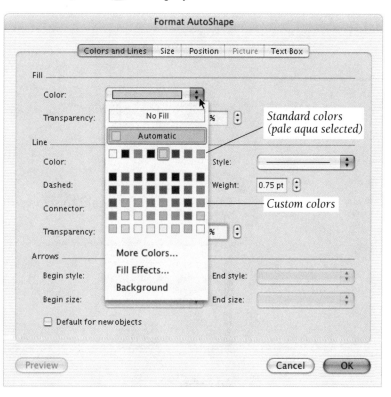

> *Colors in top row (directly under* Automatic*) of color menu are from
> standard color scheme. To add custom colors, you choose* More Colors *near
> bottom of menu. Added colors appear below standard colors.*

In group of custom colors, click sky blue color. Click **OK**.

> *Rectangle JOHN is filled with solid blue.*

3 Change fill color of rectangle VAL to pink

Select rectangle **VAL**. Follow step 2 above, except choose pink color.

Tip

*You can also double-click an object
(away from any text it contains) to
select the object for formatting and
automatically open the* Format
AutoShape *dialog box.*

Tip

You can click the Preview *button to
see the effect without closing the
dialog box. If you don't like the
result, click* Cancel. *You may have
to move the dialog box to see the
result. Press and drag the title bar
of the dialog box.*

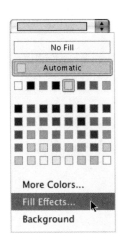

4 Change fill from solid to shaded

Double-click rectangle **SAM** (away from name).

In **Fill** area of dialog box, click ⬦ to display **Color** menu.

On menu, choose **Fill Effects**. If necessary, click **Gradient** in bar at top.

In **Shading styles** area, choose **From center**.

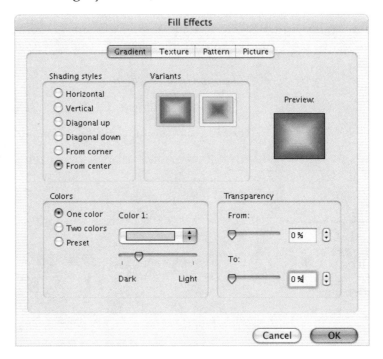

By the way

You can also change the colors by using the options in the Colors area of the dialog box. You can even use two colors.

Click **OK**, then **OK** again to see result. Click clear area of slide to deselect object.

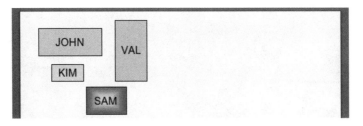

5 Add other fills

Double-click rectangle **KIM** (away from name).

In **Fill** area of dialog box, click ⬦ to display **Color** menu.

On menu, again choose **Fill Effects**.

Click **Pattern** in bar at top to see patterned fills. Choose one you like.

Click **OK** twice to see result.

Use same method to experiment with textured fills.

By the way

In patterned fills, the current fill color appears as the foreground, with white as the default background. You can use the pop-up menus to change either color.

6 Save changed file

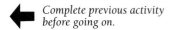
Change outline & shadow

In addition to modifying an object's fill, you can change line color, style, and pattern; and you can add and adjust a shadow.

1 Switch object outline off and back on

Select rectangle **JOHN**.

Near bottom of drawing toolbar, click arrow at right of (line color).

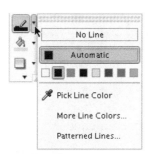

Tip

If you remove both line and fill from an object, it can "disappear." If this happens, on the Edit *menu, choose* Select All *to see the selection handles for the missing object.*

Choose **No Line**.

Outline is removed from object.

Click arrow at right of again. Choose **Automatic**.

Standard (thin black) outline is added to object.

2 Change line width of same rectangle

On drawing toolbar, click **≡ ▾** (line style). On menu, choose solid line labeled **6 pt**.

Deselect object.

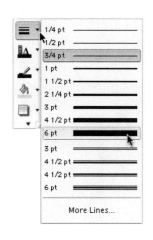

Outline of rectangle is wider. (Width you see on rectangle depends on zoom percentage setting shown on standard toolbar.)

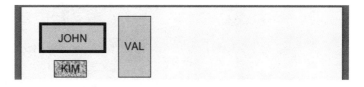

3 Change line style and dash style of rectangle VAL

Double-click rectangle **VAL** (away from name)

In **Line** area of dialog box, click **Style** pop-up menu.

On menu, choose **6 pt**.

In same area, display **Dashed** menu. Select fourth format (see figure at left).

Click **OK** to see result. Deselect object.

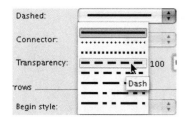

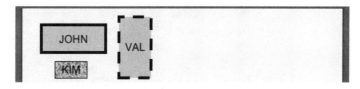

Outline is thick and dashed.

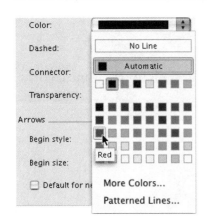

4 *Change line color*

Double-click rectangle **JOHN** (away from name).

In **Line** area of dialog box, click **Color** pop-up menu.

Choose red color. Click **OK**.

5 *Add shadow*

Select rectangle **KIM**.

At top of drawing toolbar, click  (draw). On menu, choose **Simple Shadow**. On submenu, choose **Shadow Style 6**, as in lower figure at left.

Click outside rectangle to see shadow.

6 *Change shadow color*

Select rectangle **KIM** again.

On drawing toolbar, click again. On menu, choose **Simple Shadow**. At bottom of submenu, click **Shadow Settings**.

    Shadow settings options appear on small floating toolbar.

Click arrow at right of (shadow color) to see pop-up menu.

Click black color (either one will work).

7 *Increase shadow offset*

In shadow settings toolbar, use buttons (nudge shadow) to increase or decrease offset of shadow in direction of arrow.

Click at left of shadow settings toolbar to close it.

Deselect object to see result similar to figure below.

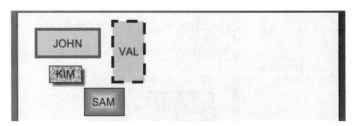

8 *Save changed Objects document; close document*

Align objects

Microsoft PowerPoint allows you to line objects up with one
another on their edges or centers.

1 *Create new presentation document with blank slide*

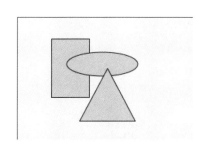

On **File** menu, choose **New Presentation**.

Use **Formatting Palette** to choose blank slide layout (see page 74, step 2)

On drawing toolbar, click ▧ ▾ (AutoShapes). Choose **Basic Shapes**. Click
double-bar at top to float as palette.

On palette, use rectangle, then oval, then triangle tools to draw objects.

Close palette. Move and resize objects as in figure at left.

2 *Align two objects along top edges*

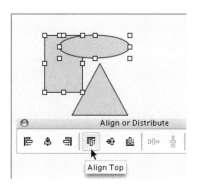

At top of drawing toolbar, click ▨ ▾ (draw). Choose **Align or Distribute**,
then click bar at top to float as palette.

Deselect all objects. With (SHIFT) held down, click rectangle and oval objects.

On palette, click ▥ (align top).

Lower object (oval) moves up so top edges are aligned.

3 *Undo alignment change*

On **Edit** menu, choose **Undo Align Object** (or click ↺ on standard toolbar).

4 *Align objects by left edges*

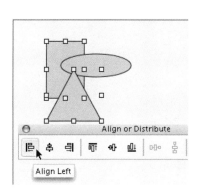

Select just rectangle and triangle.

On palette, click ▤ (align left).

Object farther to right (triangle) moves left so left edges are aligned.

5 *Undo alignment*

On **Edit** menu, choose **Undo Align Object** (or click ↺).

6 *Align objects by centers*

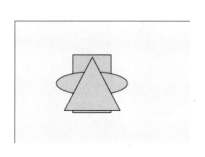

On **Edit** menu, choose **Select All** (or tap ⌘ A).

On palette, click ▤ (align center), then ▥ (align middle).

Deselect objects to see results better.

*Object in front is one you created last. (You'll learn about stacking order on
page 92.)*

7 *Undo both new alignments*

On standard toolbar, click tiny arrow at right of ↺ ▾.

On menu, click last **Align Object** item. Click outside objects to deselect all.

Objects return to positions in top figure at left.

Close **Align or Distribute** palette.

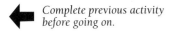
Change stacking order

Each new object is on a layer in front of the rest of the objects, but you can change the order of the layers.

1 **Notice stacking order**

Arrange objects as in figure at left. Deselect objects.

Notice stacking order.

> *Each new object you drew is on layer in front of older object(s).*

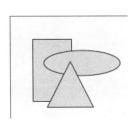

2 **Move triangle behind oval**

At top of drawing toolbar, click 🎲 ▾ (draw) to see menu.

Choose **Arrange**, then click bar at top of submenu to create palette.

> *Palette name is Order.*

Select just triangle.

> *Triangle is in front of oval and rectangle.*

On palette, click 🔳 (send backward).

> *Layer with triangle is now behind oval but still in front of rectangle.*

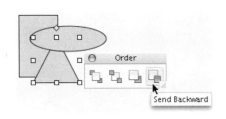

3 **Move oval layer behind all other objects**

Click oval to select it (and deselect triangle).

> *Oval is now on top of other objects.*

On palette, click 🔳 (send to back).

> *Layer with oval is now behind others.*

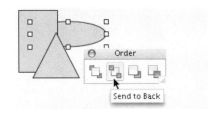

4 **Move rectangle one layer forward**

Click rectangle to select it (and deselect oval).

> *Rectangle is behind triangle, but in front of oval.*

On palette, click 🔳 (bring forward).

> *Layer with rectangle is now in front of triangle.*

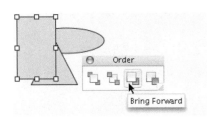

5 **Use any buttons on palette to return layers to original order**

6 **End drawing activities**

Close **Order** palette.

Close file without saving changes.

On **PowerPoint** menu, choose **Quit PowerPoint**.

If you're using floppy disk, eject it as shown on page 5, step 5.

7 **Shut down computer (see page 14, step 8)**

Presentations

Create presentation

Now that you know the main graphics tools, you'll create a slide presentation using Microsoft PowerPoint.

1 **Start computer and PowerPoint**

Switch on computer (see page 2). Do all steps on page 7, choosing **Microsoft PowerPoint** this time. (See icon on left.)

If **New Slide** dialog box appears, click **Cancel**.

2 **See Microsoft PowerPoint document window in normal view**

If necessary, make window width match figure below.

Notice three main window panes in normal view (sizes may vary).

If you have not completed activities beginning on page 74, figure may look different. You'll change that in next steps.

Menu bar ————
Standard toolbar ———
Title bar ———

View scale (yours may be different)

By the way
You'll use view buttons (lower left) to see the same presentation document in different ways.

Outline pane ———
Slide pane ———

Notes pane ———

View buttons ———

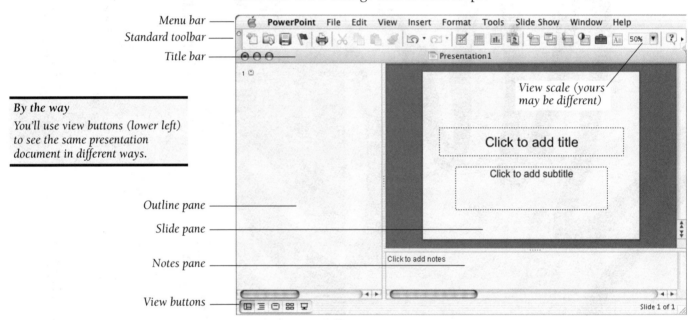

3 **Set various options as expected in this section of book**

On menu bar, click **View**.

Click as necessary so check marks appear only for **Normal** and **Formatting Palette**.

With **View** menu down, put pointer on **Toolbars**.

Click as necessary so check mark appears only for **Standard**.

If you haven't already done steps on page 75, do steps 2 and 3 now.

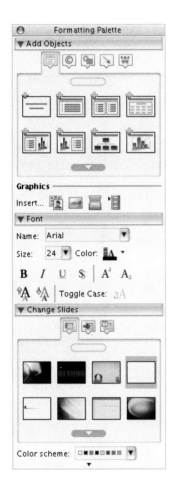

By the way

Many of the tools on the standard toolbar are identical to those on the same toolbar in other Microsoft Office applications.

4 *Find names of tools on standard toolbar*

Move pointer to each tool icon. Read name below pointer.

5 *Find names of view buttons (at bottom left of window)*

View buttons allow you to see same presentation in different ways.

6 *Notice outline pane at left of window and notes pane below slide pane*

Outline pane shows entire presentation document as outline. Notes pane is place to enter information for presenter.

7 *Notice Formatting Palette*

Point to each new tool in **Formatting Palette** to view its name.

You can add objects, change fonts, and change slide designs. (You'll learn about adding objects beginning on page 115.)

In top pane, click ▬▼▬ to see more slide layouts you can use.

In bottom pane, click ▬▼▬ to see more designs you can apply.

Changes here affect appearance of all slides in presentation document.

8 *Close Formatting Palette*

Click ⊖ on **Formatting Palette** title bar to put palette away for now.

9 *View slide 1*

Notice labels on slide 1.

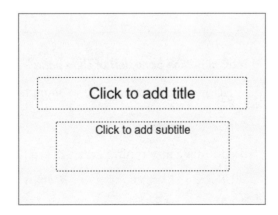

Labels are placeholders that show where objects on slides will appear. First slide is normally title slide, with place for presentation title and subtitle.

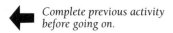
Add text to slide

Standard layouts come with placeholders for text and other objects. The next step is to replace the placeholder text.

1 **Replace title placeholder**

Click I-beam pointer anywhere inside top placeholder box on slide.

> *Text goes away, and blinking insertion point appears in box. Thick striped border means placeholder is ready for you to enter (or edit) text.*

Type Computer History Society.

Click white background area of slide, away from any text.

> *You have replaced title placeholder with your own text.*

2 **Replace subtitle placeholder**

Click I-beam pointer anywhere inside bottom placeholder box.

> *Text goes away, and insertion point appears.*

Type this: Dedicated to Remembering the Past While Moving to the Future.

> *Notice that text "wraps" (moves to next line) within margins set by box.*

Click white background area away from text box.

Tip

You can also tap RETURN *to force line breaks where you want them.*

3 **Look at slide**

> *Finished slide appears. Once placeholders are gone, slide is just like one you could have created from blank layout.*

Computer History Society

Dedicated to Remembering the
Past While Moving to the Future

---

4 **Look at outline pane, left of slide pane**

> *Title and subtitle appear as main topic and subtopic of outline.*

5 **Correct any mistakes**

If you made any typing error, move pointer over it on slide.

> *Pointer shape changes to I-beam when over text.*

Click just right of error, and make necessary corrections.

> *Tap* DELETE *to erase characters; type characters to add.*

Click white background area outside placeholders when finished.

Tip

You can also edit the text on a slide by making your changes in the outline pane.

← Complete previous activity before going on.

Save presentation

After creating a new presentation document, you should save it on a floppy or in a folder on the hard disk or network.

1 Give Save command

If using floppy disk, make sure it's in drive now.

On **File** menu, choose **Save** (or click 💾 on standard toolbar).

2 Name presentation file

Type Slides as name of file.

3 Navigate to location where you want to save document

If three panes in figure below do not appear on sheet, click ▾ at right of **Save As** text box, to see paths to locations.

If using floppy disk, click **My Disk** in top part of left pane. In middle pane, click **My Files** folder with your initials.

Name of saved document ⎯
Place to save it ⎯
Floppy disk ⎯

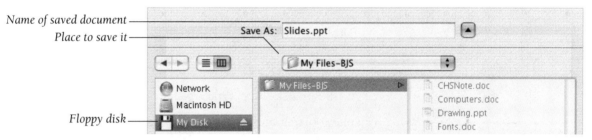

Otherwise, click **Documents** in lower part of left pane. In middle pane, click **My Files** folder with your initials.

Name of saved document ⎯
Place to save it ⎯
Folder on hard disk ⎯

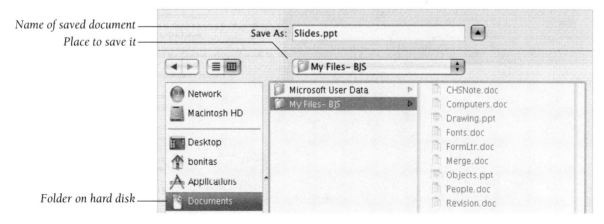

If necessary, click **Append file extension** check box to add **.ppt** to document name.

4 Save file

Click **Save** to save document with name **Slides**.

> *Title bar now shows new file name. In future, you can save changes by giving Save command. No dialog box will appear; changed file replaces original.*

By the way

A file extension shows what application program created the file: .doc for Word, .ppt for PowerPoint, etc. Macintosh applications don't need extensions to know the creator, but Windows applications do. If you add the extension, you can transfer a file to a Windows PC and continue working on it with the Windows version of the Microsoft Office applications.

Add new slide

Slides in a PowerPoint presentation are like pages in a Word document, except that you must add each slide manually.

1 Add new slide

On **Insert** menu, choose **New Slide** (or click on standard toolbar).

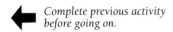

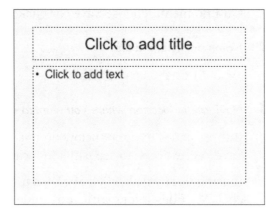

Layout of new slide is bulleted list. It has title at top and bulleted text below. This is usually what you want. You'll learn to use other layouts later.

2 Enter text for slide 2

Click title placeholder; type Welcome .

Click text placeholder; type What Can the Computer History Society Do for You?

Tap RETURN now to start new paragraph in text box.

Type your name, comma, space, and President .

> *Each paragraph has bullet mark to left.*

By the way

If a small lightbulb appears at the left of the text, click it. This is a tip about capitalization. Click Don't show me this tip again; then click OK.

3 View slide 2

Click in white area outside both text boxes.

Welcome

- What Can the Computer History Society Do for You?
- Bonita Sebastian, President

4 Correct any errors

> *You may edit text in outline pane or slide pane.*

5 Save file with new slide

On **File** menu, choose **Save** (or click 🖫 on standard toolbar).

> *No dialog box appears this time. Changed presentation file replaces previously saved version in your My Files folder. Original is permanently erased!*

Use outline view

If many of your slides will be bulleted or numbered lists, you can add and edit them easily in outline view.

1 Change to outline view

Click ☰ (outline view) at lower left of window.

Outline view is same as normal, except outline pane is wider, and slide and notes panes are smaller. If text is too small, you can use zoom pop-up menu on toolbar to increase view percentage.

Look at current outline of slide presentation. (Line breaks may vary.)

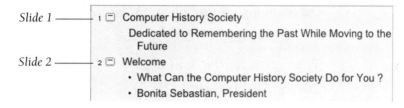

Slide 1 ——— 1 ⊟ Computer History Society
Dedicated to Remembering the Past While Moving to the Future

Slide 2 ——— 2 ⊟ Welcome
• What Can the Computer History Society Do for You ?
• Bonita Sebastian, President

2 Add slide

Click at right of **t** in **President** to position insertion point.

On **Insert** menu, choose **New Slide** (or click 🗐 on standard toolbar).

Icon for slide 3 appears in outline. Insertion point is ready for title.

3 Enter title on slide 3 in outline view

Type **Topics** and tap RETURN.

Oops! New slide 4 is automatically added, but you haven't added bulleted list for slide 3 yet!

4 Use Outlining toolbar to add bulleted list for slide 3

On **View** menu, choose **Toolbars**, then **Outlining**.

On toolbar that appears, click 🔲 (increase indent), or tap TAB.

Slide 4 icon is gone. Bullet appears, and insertion point moves to right.

Type **Introductions** and tap RETURN.

Insertion point moves down to next line at same indent level.

Type **Benefits of Membership** RETURN **Services We Provide** RETURN.

Type **Plans for the Future**. Do *not* tap RETURN now.

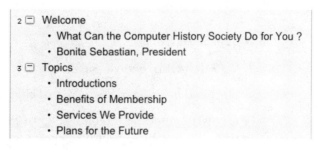

2 ⊟ Welcome
• What Can the Computer History Society Do for You ?
• Bonita Sebastian, President
3 ⊟ Topics
• Introductions
• Benefits of Membership
• Services We Provide
• Plans for the Future

5 *View text on slide 3*

Notice same text on slide 3 in small slide pane to right of outline pane.

6 *Create slide 4*

Tap [RETURN].

Oops again! New bulleted item appears. You wanted new slide.

On outlining toolbar, click [icon] (decrease indent), or tap [SHIFT][TAB].

Slide 4 appears. Bullet is gone, and insertion point moves left.

Type Introductions as title.

Tap [RETURN]; then click [icon] (increase indent), or tap [TAB].

Using methods in step 4, add bulleted list below.

> 4 ⊟ Introductions
> - Officers
> - Founding Members
> - Committee Chairs
> - New Members

7 *Create slides 5 and 6*

Using same methods, create slides 5 and 6 in outline view.

> 5 ⊟ Benefits of Membership
> - Networking Opportunities
> - Fascinating Presentations
> - Leading-Edge Speakers
> - Low Dues
> - Discounts on Training Classes
> 6 ⊟ Services We Provide
> - Computer History Archives
> - Community Assistance Job Bank
> - Low-Cost Training Classes
> - Informative Monthly Newsletter|

8 *Return to normal view, and see results on larger slide*

In group of view buttons at bottom of window, click [icon] (normal view).

9 *Close outlining toolbar*

10 *Save Slides file*

On **File** menu, choose **Save**.

You'll be using file you created many times in future activities.

If you're not going on, choose **Quit PowerPoint** on **PowerPoint** menu. If using floppy disk, eject it as shown on page 5, step 5.

Tip

It's a good idea to use outline view when you're creating a new presentation. Outline view lets you focus on the information you want to get across. You can decide on appearances later.

STOP *Slides file as saved on page 100 must be available.*

View slides

There are two ways to see the slides themselves: switch to slide view or to slide show view. You'll explore both now.

By the way
The normal and outline views differ in only one respect: the positions of the dividers that separate the outline, the slide, and the notes panes. In either view, you can drag the dividers to change the spacing.

1 *View presentation in slide view*

If necessary, start Microsoft PowerPoint, and open **Slides** presentation.

In group of view buttons at bottom of window, click ▭ (slide view).

In slide view, outline pane and notes pane disappear.

2 *Move to last slide in presentation*

Tap [⌘][END] (or [FN][⌘][END] on laptop).

Laptop users need to hold down [FN] to change function of arrow keys to [END], [HOME], [PAGE UP], and [PAGE DOWN].

3 *Move directly to first slide*

Tap [⌘][HOME].

These commands work same way in all Microsoft Office applications.

4 *View slides one by one (method 1)*

Tap [PAGE DOWN] to move to next slide; tap [PAGE UP] to see previous slide.

5 *View slides one by one (method 2)*

Click next slide button (below vertical scroll bar).

⬧—— *Previous slide*
⬧—— *Next slide*

Continue to click next slide button until you reach last slide.

Click previous slide button on vertical scroll bar.

Next to last slide appears.

6 *Use scroll box to move to slide 1*

Press and hold scroll box. Notice slide indicator near scroll box.

Slide 5. Benefits of Membership

Watch indicator as you drag scroll box slowly to top of scroll bar.

7 *View slide show*

By the way
A slide show on your monitor is just one way to use your presentation. You can also make color or black-and-white overhead transparencies. You can even use the presentation to make 35mm slides. If you're in a hurry to learn about this, skip to page 125.

At bottom of window, click ▱ (slide show) view button.

Presentation begins, with current slide filling whole screen. You can't edit text in this view.

Tap spacebar, [↓], or [TAB], or click to see next slide. Do it again.

Tap [↑] or [SHIFT][TAB] to see previous slide.

Move forward through all slides until slide view returns.

Add dynamic effects

You can add transitions and animations to a presentation
viewed on a computer monitor or through a projection device.

1 Switch to slide sorter view

If necessary, open file **Slides**. At bottom of window, click ⊞ (slide sorter view).

You see all slides as if on light table. Slide sorter toolbar appears at top.

Put pointer on each tool in slide sorter toolbar to see its name.

2 Explore transition effects

If necessary, click slide 1 to select it.

At left of new toolbar, click ⬊ (slide transition) to see dialog box.

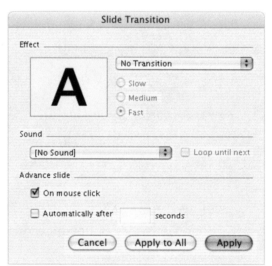

In **Effect** area, click ⬦ to see pop-up menu of possible transition effects.

Watch figure at top as you choose **Blinds Horizontal** from list.

Figure shows how effect works when slide first appears in show.

3 Add transition effect to slide 1

On same pop-up menu, choose **Split Vertical Out**. For timing option, click **Slow** radio button.

Click **Apply** (*not* Apply to All!).

Notice name of transition on toolbar.

4 Add different transition to slide 2

Click slide 2 image.

On slide sorter toolbar, use transition pop-up menu to choose **Fade Through Black**.

5   *Add transitions to many slides at once*

Click slide 3 image.

With (SHIFT) held down, click slide 6.

> *Slides 3, 4, 5, and 6 are selected.*

On toolbar, click 🔁 to display **Slide Transition** dialog box.

On **Effect** pop-up menu, choose **Wipe Left**.

Choose **Medium** for timing option.

Click **Apply**.

6   *Add animation effect to objects on slides*

If necessary, select slides 3, 4, 5, and 6.

On **Slide Show** menu, choose **Preset Animations**, then **Fly In**.

7   *View slide show with effects*

Select slide 1. Click 🖵 (slide show) at bottom of window.

> *Screen opens black, then splits vertically to reveal slide 1.*

Move mouse around. Click 🔲▲ when it appears at lower left.

On pop-up menu, choose **Pointer Options**; from submenu, choose **Pen**.

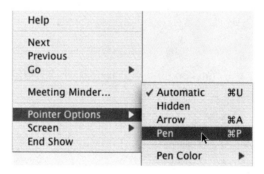

Use mouse to draw line under title.

Tap spacebar, (↓), or (TAB) to move to next slide.

> *Screen fades from black through to slide 2.*

Go forward through whole slide show.

> *You may hear sound added with animation. Animation makes slides 3, 4, 5, and 6 grow bullet by bullet on screen as you advance.*

8   *Close presentation file without saving changes*

On **File** menu, choose **Close**.

Click **Don't Save** when asked whether to save changes.

Tip

You can go directly to any slide by typing the slide number and tapping (RETURN). You can end a slide show anytime by tapping (ESC).

Check spelling

Microsoft PowerPoint can check the spelling in a presentation and add new words to your custom dictionary.

1 **Open file Slides in normal view**

2 **Begin spelling check**

On **Tools** menu, choose **Spelling**.

If Microsoft PowerPoint detects errors, Spelling dialog box appears.

By the way

If no words are misspelled, the Spelling dialog box does not open at all. Only the message box in step 5 appears.

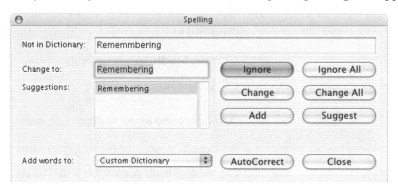

3 **Change any misspelled words**

In **Suggestions** list, click to highlight desired replacement word.

Click **Change**.

You can click Change All to replace all occurrences of misspelled word in entire presentation.

4 **Work with flagged proper names**

If your name is flagged by spelling checker, click **Ignore**.

You can click Ignore All to skip other occurrences of flagged word in entire presentation.

OR

Click **Add** to include your name in custom dictionary so it will never be flagged again.

5 **End spelling check**

When spelling check is finished, message below appears.

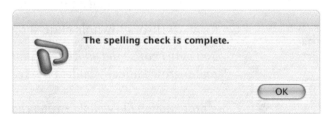

Click **OK**.

6 **Save presentation file with changes**

On **File** menu, choose **Save**.

Edit & rearrange text

You can edit text in normal, slide, or outline view. You can also easily rearrange the order of bullets on a slide in these views.

1 **If necessary, open Slides file**

2 **Edit text on slide 1 in slide view**

Click ⬜ (slide view) at lower left of window.

If necessary, navigate to slide 1.

Double-click to select word **Moving**.

Type Racing.

> Racing *replaces* Moving. *Slide 1 should now look like figure below.*

Computer History Society

Dedicated to Remembering the Past While Racing to the Future

3 **Change to outline view**

Click ☰ (outline view).

> *Change you made appears in every view.*

4 **Rearrange bulleted lines on slide 2 in outline view**

Click in bulleted line containing your name.

Position pointer to left of bullet mark at left side of text.

Watch for pointer to change shape: ✛ Bonita Sebastian, President .

Press and drag up to move text under title of slide.

2 🖻 Welcome
    What Can the Computer History Society Do for You?
    • Bonita Sebastian, President

> *Horizontal line across pane marks new location of highlighted text.*

When line is at correct location, release mouse button.

> *Highlighted line moves to new location.*

5 **Add bulleted line to slide 2 in outline view**

Click to right of **You?** in second bulleted line. Tap RETURN.

> *New line at same outline level is created when you tap* RETURN.

Type this: What Can You Do for the Computer History Society?

Tip

You can also move lines up or down with the move-up and move-down tools on the outlining toolbar. If the toolbar is hidden, use the View *menu to see it.*

6   **Add new level of bullets to slide 5**

In outline view, locate slide 5.

Click to put insertion point just right of **Low Dues**. Tap RETURN.

New bulleted line at same level is created.

If necessary, use **Toolbars** command on **View** menu to show outlining toolbar.

On toolbar, click [icon] (increase indent), or tap TAB.

New line is indented one level.

Type Regular $50/year and tap RETURN.

Another bulleted line at new level is created. RETURN *always creates new line at same level as line above.*

Enter remaining line as shown in figure. Don't tap RETURN after last line.

> 5 ⊟ Benefits of Membership
> • Networking Opportunities
> • Fascinating Presentations
> • Leading-Edge Speakers
> • Low Dues
>   • Regular $50/year
>   • Student or Senior $25/year
> • Discounts on Training Classes

7   **Close outlining toolbar**

8   **Review edited presentation in normal view**

Click [icon] to change to normal view.

Current slide appears in slide pane.

Notice indentation and bullets.

> ## Benefits of Membership
>
> • Networking Opportunities
> • Fascinating Presentations
> • Leading-Edge Speakers
> • Low Dues
>   – Regular $50/year
>   – Student or Senior $25/year
> • Discounts on Training Classes

Tap ⌘ HOME to move to slide 1. Click [icon] (next slide) to browse though slides one by one.

9   **Close presentation file without saving changes**

Rearrange slides

After reviewing slides, you may wish to rearrange the order in which information is presented.

1 Open Slides file

2 Switch to slide sorter view

Click ⊞ (slide sorter view) at bottom left of window.

Slides appear in miniature, as if on light table.

By the way

Your screen may not look exactly like this one. The display will depend on the size of your monitor and the current view percentage.

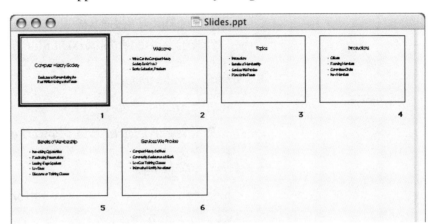

3 Change order of slides (method 1)

Put pointer in slide 3; drag to left of slide 2.

Notice vertical position marker near pointer.

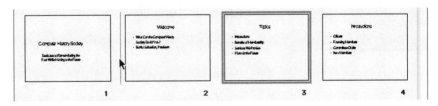

When position marker is to left of slide 2, release mouse button.

Slide 3 (Topics) becomes slide 2. Slide 2 (Welcome) becomes slide 3.

4 Change order of slides (method 2)

Click ☰ (outline view) at bottom left of window.

Outline shows new order. Order of slides is same in all views.

Put pointer at small slide icon to left of slide 3 title: ₃⊕ Welcome .

Press mouse button, and drag up until long horizontal position marker is just above slide 2 title.

Release mouse button.

Highlighted text moves up to marker. Welcome is now slide 2 again.

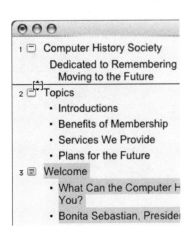

5 If you're not continuing, close Slides presentation file without saving changes

If you're not going on, choose **Quit PowerPoint** on **PowerPoint** menu. If using floppy disk, eject it as shown on page 5, step 5.

Delete slide

Sometimes you simply want to get rid of a slide in your presentation. That's easy to do (and undo).

1 **If necessary, start PowerPoint and open Slides file**

2 **Delete slide (method 1)**

If necessary, click 📄 to switch to outline view.

Click icon for slide 3 to select all text on slide.

On **Edit** menu, choose **Clear**.

> *Slide is deleted from presentation file.*

3 **Undo action (method 1)**

On **Edit** menu, choose **Undo Clear**.

> *Slide is "undeleted." Most PowerPoint actions can be undone.*

4 **Delete slide (method 2)**

Click ▦ (slide sorter view) at bottom left of window.

Make sure slide 3 is selected.

Tap DELETE.

> *Slide 3 is deleted, and other slides are renumbered.*

By the way

You can click the arrow on the side of the undo tool to display a list of recent actions you can undo.

5 **Undo action (method 2)**

Click ↺ (undo) on standard toolbar.

> *Slide 3 reappears, still selected.*

6 **Delete slide (method 3)**

Click ▭ (slide view) at bottom left of window.

> *Selected slide fills window.*

On **Edit** menu, choose **Delete Slide**.

> *Delete Slide command can be used in any view. It always deletes selected slide(s).*

7 **Undo action (method 3)**

Tap ⌘ Z.

> *Slide 3 reappears.*

8 **Close Slides file without saving changes**

Slides file as saved on page 100 (or later) must be available.

Change text formats

You can easily change the font, size, and style of any text you select on a slide.

1 Open Slides file

2 View slide 1 in normal view

If necessary, click  to switch to normal view. Tap ⌘ HOME to see slide 1.

3 Display Formatting Palette

On **View** menu, choose **Formatting Palette**, or click ▣ on standard toolbar.

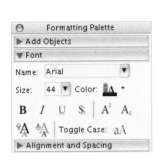

4 Check current font, size, and style of title

In slide pane, highlight any text in title.

In **Font** pane of **Formatting Palette**, view current font (**Arial**), size (**44** point), style (none—no bold, italic, underline, or shadow), and color (black).

5 Change font, size, and style of title

Triple-click title to select whole line.

On **Name** pop-up menu on palette, choose font you like.

Click **B** (bold), then *I* (italic), then **$** (shadow).

On size pop-up menu, choose **60**.

Changes affect only highlighted text. Title may wrap to second line.

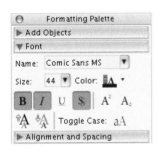

Below style buttons, click ⁺A (decrease font size) until title is on one line.

6 Change all text in subtitle

Click slide away from any text.

Tap TAB twice to select subtitle block.

Thick patterned border shows whole text block is selected.

Use method above to change font to one you like.

Click **B**.

All text in selected block is changed.

By the way

Applying format changes directly to a slide is called "custom formatting." On page 110, you'll learn a simple way to make format changes to all slides at once.

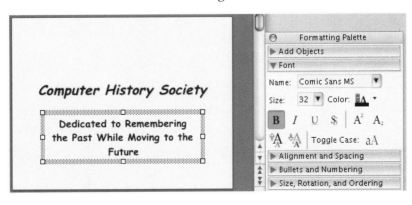

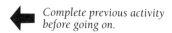

Complete previous activity before going on.

Use slide master

Every presentation has a "slide master." Format changes you make on the slide master affect all similar slides.

Switch to view of slide master

Go to slide 4. Click ⬜ to switch to slide view.

On **View** menu, choose **Master**, then **Slide Master**.

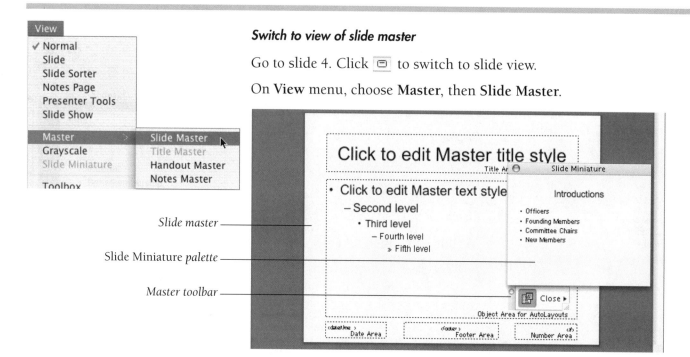

Slide master ⎯

Slide Miniature *palette* ⎯

Master toolbar ⎯

Slide master has formatting placeholders that affect most other slides. Small master toolbar and Slide Miniature palette also appear.

2 Format title placeholder on slide master

Click text inside top text box. Notice striped border.

Use **Formatting Palette** to change font and add bold, italic, and shadow styles.

3 Format body text placeholder on slide master

Click border of body text. Notice dotted border.

Change all text in box to font you like with bold style.

4 Change size of some text within body

Click anywhere in first bulleted line. Notice striped border.

Use **Formatting Palette** to change font size to **28**.

Text size is changed for first-level items only.

5 See results

Tap ⌘ HOME to go to first slide. Click 🖥 to view slide show. Notice text format of each slide.

All slides except slide 1 now have formats you gave to slide master. (You gave slide 1 custom formats in previous activity, so it is unchanged.)

On tiny master toolbar, click Close to leave slide master view.

6 Close Slides presentation file without saving changes

Tip

Pay attention to borders. A striped border means that text you clicked inside the box is selected for formatting. A dotted border means the whole text box is selected.

Tip

Do most of your formatting in slide master view instead of formatting each slide separately. Later, if you decide on a design change, all you have to do is change the master.

STOP Slides *file as saved on page 100 (or later) must be available.*

Add slide with chart

You can add a chart to a slide. Creating a chart in Microsoft PowerPoint is similar to creating one in Microsoft Excel.

1 **Open Slides file in normal view**

2 **Add new slide with chart layout**

Tap ⌘ END to go to last slide.

In **Add Objects** pane of **Formatting Palette**, click layout in figure.

New slide appears with layout for chart.

Tip
You can also add a chart to any slide by using the Chart command on the Insert menu.

3 **Add title**

Click title placeholder; type Computers in Use.

4 **Start Microsoft Graph application**

On slide, double-click chart placeholder.

In time, Graph in Slides *windows appear. They belong to Microsoft Graph application.*

Look at names in menu bar near top of screen. Look at toolbars.

Data and Chart menus are new. Slide Show menu is gone. Items on menus are also changed. Menu bar and toolbars now belong to Microsoft Graph.

On **View** menu, choose **Datasheet** (now unchecked).

Double click to add chart

Tip
Do not click a window behind the Graph in Slides windows. If you do, you will return to the Microsoft PowerPoint application. If this happens, double-click the chart to return to the Microsoft Graph application.

Graph in Slides - Datasheet *window becomes active. You see default data.*

		A	B	C	D	E	F	G
		1st Qtr	2nd Qtr	3rd Qtr	4th Qtr			
1	East	20.4	27.4	90	20.4			
2	West	30.6	38.6	34.6	31.6			
3	North	45.9	46.9	45	43.9			
4								

Graph in Slides.ppt – Datasheet

5 **Enter new column labels**

Click to select cell in row 1 containing word **East**.

Type Business and tap RETURN.

Active cell is now West.

Type School and tap RETURN.

Active cell is now North.

Type Home and tap RETURN.

In window with chart, notice new names in legend to right of chart.

6 *Enter new row labels*

Click to select cell containing words **1st Qtr.**

Type **1990** and tap TAB.

   Active cell is now 2nd Qtr.

Type **1995** and tap TAB to move to next cell to right.

Type **2000** and tap TAB to end text entry.

By the way

As you make changes in the data-sheet, they are reflected in the chart.

7 *Remove column D data from chart*

Double-click ⬚ D ⬚ (header of column D).

   Data are dimmed in window and disappear from chart.

8 *Enter new data*

By the way

The numbers used in this example are simply figures for the exercise and bear no relation to the actual numbers (which are much larger).

Beginning in cell A1, enter new data shown in figure.

		A	B	C	D	E	F	G
		1990	1995	2000	4thQtr			
1	Business	50,000	70,000	98,000	20.4			
2	School	20,000	35,000	87,000	31.6			
3	Home	10,000	25,000	60,000	43.9			

Graph in Slides.ppt - Datasheet

9 *View results in Microsoft Graph*

On **View** menu, choose **Datasheet** (now checked).

   Graph in Slides - Chart window becomes active.

10 *View results in Microsoft PowerPoint*

On **Graph** menu, choose **Quit & Return to Slides.**

   PowerPoint menus and toolbars reappear. Changed chart is on slide.

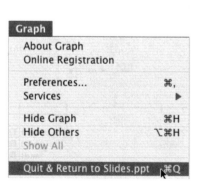

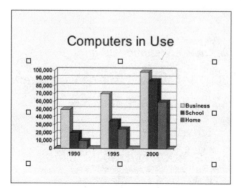

Click 🖥 to see result in slide show. Tap ESC to end show.

11 *Save presentation file*

On **File** menu, choose **Save.**

Format chart

Charts in Microsoft PowerPoint can be formatted using methods similar to those used in Microsoft Excel.

1 Start Microsoft Graph

On slide, double-click anywhere inside chart area.

In time, Microsoft Graph toolbars and menus appear.

2 Add label to value axis

On **Chart** menu, choose **Chart Options**.

Click text box for **Value (Z) axis**.

Type Computers.

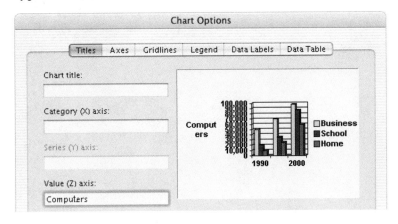

Click **OK**.

New Computers *label appears in* Graph in Slides - Chart *window.*

3 Format axis title

Make sure new label box is selected.

On **Format** menu, choose **Selected Axis Title**.

In **Format Axis Title** dialog box, click **Alignment** in bar at top.

In **Orientation** area, drag red diamond to top (see figure below).

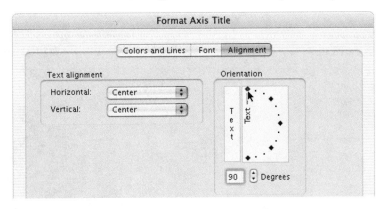

Click **OK**.

4   *Move legend to bottom*

Double-click legend (at right of chart).

Format Legend *dialog box appears.*

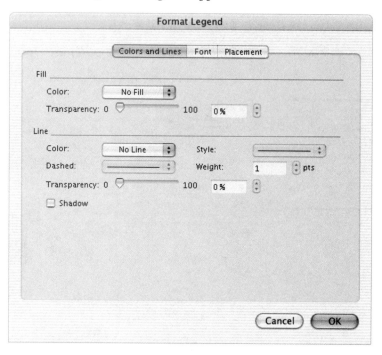

Click **Placement** in bar at top. In **Type** area, click **Bottom**.

Click OK.

5   *Change data being graphed*

On **View** menu, choose **Datasheet** to activate window.

Click cell C3 containing **60,000** (home computers used in 2000).

Type 100,000 and tap (RETURN).

6   *View finished chart on slide*

Quit Microsoft Graph and return to **Slides** presentation.

By the way

The chart is now an object on the slide. It can be deleted, moved, or resized by applying the same techniques used with other graphic objects. See page 78.

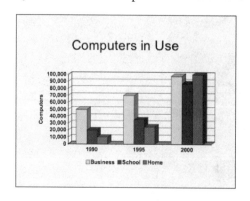

7   *Save presentation with new slide*

Add clip art

You can add a graphic object to a slide. Microsoft PowerPoint contains a gallery of clip art that you can use.

Tip

You can also add clip art to any slide by using the Picture *command on the* Insert *menu. See step 7.*

By the way

The amount of clip art displayed in the gallery is determined by the installation. If you do not have the entire collection, substitute other images.

The first time the Clip Gallery is opened, a dialog box may appear asking whether to add new images. If this happens, you can say yes. Be aware, however, that the process takes time.

1 **If necessary, open Slides file in slide view**

2 **Create new slide**

In **Add Objects** pane of **Formatting Palette**, choose layout in figure at left.

New slide appears with different layout.

Notice clip art placeholder at right and bulleted text box at left.

Click title placeholder. Type `Computers for All`.

3 **Open and view Clip Gallery**

Double-click clip art placeholder.

Microsoft Clip Gallery appears.

Scroll through categories that appear.

4 **Find image**

If necessary, highlight text in **Search** text box at top. Type `computer` and click **Search** button.

Review images. Click one you like.

5   *Insert picture*

Click **Insert** to accept clip art and add it to slide.

By the way

The clip art is now an object on the slide. It can be deleted, moved, or resized by applying the same techniques used with other objects. See page 78.

Tip

If the Picture toolbar does not appear when you select the clip art image, use the Toolbars submenu on the View menu to display it.

6   *View Picture toolbar*

> *Picture toolbar contains buttons for modifying picture.*

With image selected, put pointer on each button, and read description.

> *You can resize, recolor, rotate, add shadow, and much more.*

7   *Add clip art to existing slide (without clip art placeholder)*

In **Slides** file, go to slide 2.

On **Insert** menu, choose **Picture**, then **Clip Art**.

Use steps 2 and 3 to find and insert picture of people or computer.

Once image is on slide, adjust its size, and move it to desired location.

> *Finished slide should look similar to figure below.*

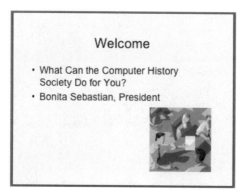

Close **Picture** toolbar.

8   *Save presentation*

STOP Slides file as saved on page 100 *(or later) must be available.*

Insert WordArt

You can add a text graphic to a slide. Microsoft Office includes a WordArt application for this.

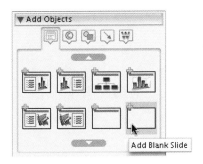

1 *If necessary, open Slides file in slide view*

2 *Add new blank slide*

Tap ⌘ END to go to last slide.

At bottom of **Add Objects** pane of **Formatting Palette**, click ⬛⬛⬛ .

In new layouts, choose blank slide as in figure at left.

3 *Add WordArt to slide*

On **Insert** menu, choose **Picture**, then **WordArt**.

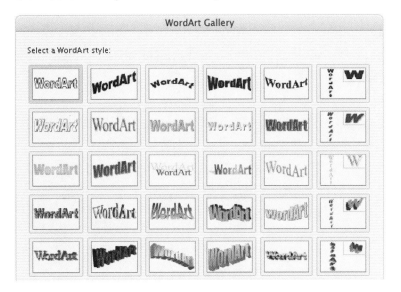

Choose style in fourth row, fourth column. Click **OK**.

By the way

The WordArt text becomes an object on the slide. The text cannot be edited without returning to WordArt. The object can be deleted, moved, and resized by applying the same techniques used with other objects. See page 78.

4 *Add text*

Type Computer History Society .

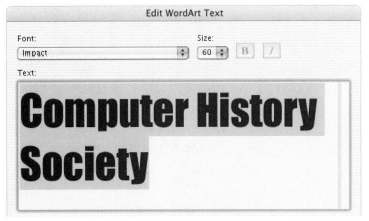

Click **OK**. Explore yellow handles on resulting WordArt object.

Explore tools on **WordArt** toolbar. Then close toolbar.

5 *Save changed presentation*

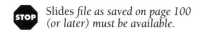
Add objects to master

Frequently you want a label or a graphic on all slides in a presentation. Just add the item to the slide master.

1 *If necessary, open Slides file in slide view*

2 *Go to slide master view*

On **View** menu, choose **Master**, then **Slide Master**.

If necessary, enlarge window so text at bottom of master is legible.

Tip

You can also move to the slide master by holding down [SHIFT] *and clicking the slide view button at the bottom of the window.*

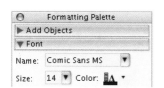

3 *Enter text*

At bottom of master, double-click **<footer>** inside **Footer Area** text box.

Type Computer History Society.

4 *Format text*

Press and drag to select all text you just typed.

On **Formatting Palette**, choose font you like. Click *I* (italic).

5 *View text on slides*

At bottom of window, click 🖳 (normal view).

Go to slide 1. Notice new footer text at bottom.

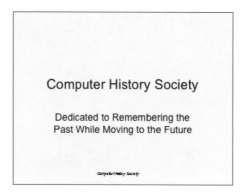

Click title, then subtitle to select text boxes. Try selecting footer box.

You can't select footer box; it's on slide master.

Click 🖵 to see slide show. Notice same footer on each slide.

6 *Switch back to slide master view*

On **View** menu, choose **Master**, then **Slide Master**.

7 *Add graphic object to slide master*

On **Insert** menu, choose **Picture**, then **Clip Art**.

Use steps 3–5 on pages 115–116 to locate and insert appropriate graphic image.

8 *Resize and position object in upper-right corner*

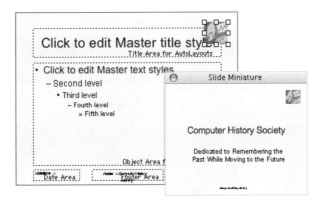

9 *View text and graphic object on all slides*

Click 🖳 to return to normal view.

Try to select new graphic object on slide.

You can't do it. Object is on slide master.

Click 🖵 to see slide show. Notice that same object appears on each slide.

10 *Suppress display of slide master objects on one slide*

If necessary, move to slide 1.

On **Format** menu, choose **Slide Background**.

Click **Omit background graphics from master** to put mark in check box.

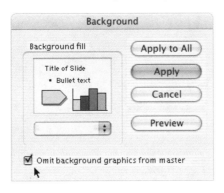

Click **Apply** (*not* Apply to All).

11 *View presentation using slide show*

Click 🖵 to see slide show.

Notice that object and footer are missing from slide 1.

12 *When show has ended, close presentation without saving changes*

Tip

A better method of formatting title slides is to use the title master view. Formats you apply there affect all slides that use the Title *layout. First, go to such a slide in slide view. Then, on the* View *menu, choose* Master, *then* Title Master. *(Bug alert! This feature is dimmed out and unavailable in the initial release of the software.)*

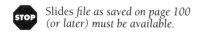 Slides *file as saved on page 100 (or later) must be available.*

Change color scheme

Background, text, and objects have their own standard colors, but you can easily switch standards. All slides adapt.

1 *Open Slides presentation file*

2 *Learn about color schemes*

On **Format** menu, choose **Slide Color Scheme**.

Blue border shows current scheme applied to whole presentation.

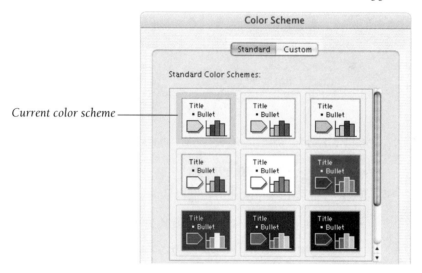

Current color scheme —

Click **Custom** in bar at top to see how items are colored in this scheme.

Labels show how standard parts of slides are now colored.

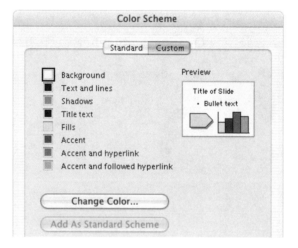

By the way

By clicking one of the colors and then the Change Color button, you can modify a scheme. You can also save the changed scheme without eliminating the original.

3 *Change color schemes*

Click **Standard** in bar at top. Click color scheme with dark background.

Click **Custom** in bar to see how items would be colored in this scheme.

Click **Apply to All**. Click 🖳 to see slide show.

By the way

Changing the color scheme has no effect on clip art, WordArt objects, or objects that you have given a custom color to.

4 *Use steps 2 and 3 to try other color schemes*

5 *Close presentation file without saving changes*

Apply design template

Microsoft PowerPoint contains built-in color and black-and-white templates you can apply to presentation files.

1 Open Slides file

2 View available presentation templates

On **Format** menu, choose **Slide Design**.

Click design name in right pane to see sample of design.

> *List moves to middle pane; preview of selected template appears at right.*

Use ↓ and ↑ to scroll through list of available templates.

3 Apply template

Choose name of template you want to use. Click **Apply**.

> *Effect is to replace your slide master, title master, and color schemes with ones from template file.*

4 View presentation with new design elements

On **View** menu, choose **Slide Show** (or click 🖥).

> *If you do not like template, you can follow steps 2 and 3 to apply another one. New template items erase previous ones.*

5 Save presentation as new file

On **File** menu, choose **Save As** (*not* Save).

Save with name **Slides with Design** in your **My Files** folder.

> *Original file without template remains in folder.*

6 Close presentation file

Tip

You can also use the first button on the Add Objects *pane of the Formatting Palette to apply these same designs.*

Tip

It's usually a good idea to keep a copy of a presentation without a template. That makes it easier to go back and make changes.

Create speaker notes

Each slide has a speaker notes page where you can write anything you want to be reminded of during the presentation.

1 Open file Slides

2 Enter speaker notes for slide 1

If necessary, click 🔲 to go to normal view.

Put pointer on split bar below slide pane. Drag up about 1 inch.

After dragging, notes pane should look like figure below.

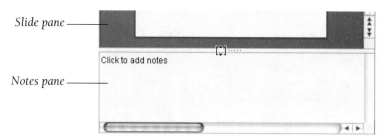

Slide pane ————

Notes pane ————

Click text placeholder in notes pane.

Type following text. Tap RETURN after first sentence.

This first slide should be displayed as the audience enters. Take a deep breath, and count to 10 before proceeding.

3 See preview of printed notes page

On **View** menu, choose **Notes Page**. Notice reduced view scale.

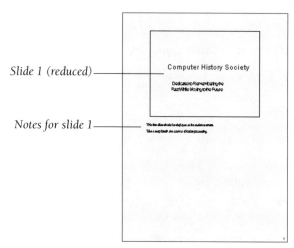

Slide 1 (reduced) ————

Notes for slide 1 ————

Click ⬇ (next slide) or tap PAGE DOWN to see next slide.

Notice notes area, ready for text.

You can enter notes directly in this view, but you'd need to enlarge view scale to read type. Entry is simplest in normal view.

Go back to slide 1.

4 Show Formatting Palette, if necessary

On **View** menu, choose **Formatting Palette** if it's not already checked.

By the way

You would not use speaker notes on the screen, of course. You print them and use the printed copy during your presentation. See page 126 for details of printing.

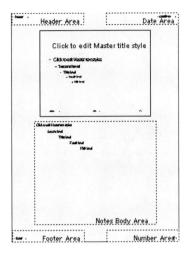

5 **Use notes master to format all notes pages**

On **View** menu, choose **Master**, then **Notes Master**.

Just as slide master can change appearance of all slides (see page 110), notes master can control appearance of all notes pages.

On notes master, carefully click border of lower text block.

In **Font** pane of **Formatting Palette**, choose **18** on **Size** pop-up menu.

On **View** menu, choose **Notes Page**. Notice larger type in notes.

6 **Add header and footer information to all notes pages**

On **View** menu, choose **Header and Footer**.

In dialog box, Notes and Handouts *is selected in bar at top.*

In **Date and time** area, click **Update automatically**.

In **Header** text box, type Computer History Society .

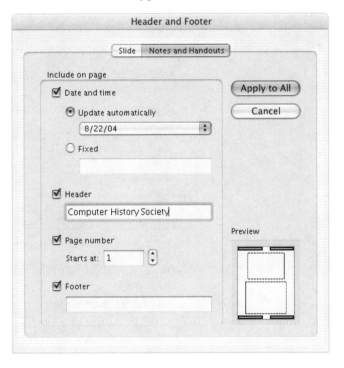

By the way

Changes made in this dialog box affect notes pages and also audience handouts (see page 124).

By the way

You can also enter a date, header, page number, and footer directly on the notes master, with results appearing on all pages. The dialog box lets you specify that the date should be updated automatically.

Click **Apply to All**. Notice changes on page.

Click ⬇ to see other pages.

Changes you made affected all notes pages.

Tap ⌘ HOME to move to page 1 of notes.

7 **Rename, save, and close presentation file**

On **File** menu, choose **Save As**. Save file with name **Notes** in your **My Files** folder.

On **File** menu, choose **Close**.

Create audience handouts

To assist note takers, you can create audience handouts with two, three, four, six, or nine slide miniatures on a page.

1 Open Slides file

2 View handout master

On **View** menu, choose **Master**, then **Handout Master**.

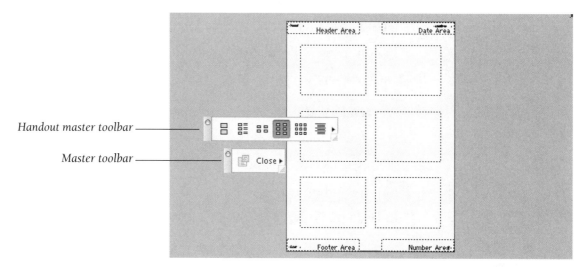

Handout master toolbar

Master toolbar

Changes you make on handout master affect all handout pages when they're printed. (You can't preview individual handout pages on screen.)

3 View different slide layouts on handout pages

Click each button on handout master toolbar to see different slide layouts.

Show positioning of 2-per-page handouts

Second button leaves space for viewers to take notes during presentation. Last button replaces slides with compact outline of presentation text.

Choose layout like one in figure at top of page.

4 Add header and footer information

Use procedure on page 123, step 6.

5 Rename, save, and close presentation file

On master toolbar, click Close to leave handout master view.

On **File** menu, choose **Save As**.

Save file with name **Handouts** in your **My Files** folder.

On **File** menu, choose **Close**.

On page 126, you'll learn how to print your notes pages and audience handouts.

STOP Slides *file as saved on page 100 (or later) must be available.*

Print overheads

With transparency film in your printer, you can print overhead slides. You can also create a file for making 35mm slides.

1 **Open Slides file**

2 **Choose general print options**

Tip

If your printer often jams when transparency film is used, print your slides on paper. Then copy them onto transparency film, using a photocopier.

On **File** menu, choose **Print**.

In **Copies** text box, type number.

If you're printing several copies and want each complete copy separated from next one, click **Collated**.

3 **Choose PowerPoint print options**

In **Slides** area, select **All** or enter range.

On pop-up menu to right of **Print What**, choose **Slides**.

On **Output**, choose **Color**, **Grayscale** *(which includes black, white, and gray)*, or **Black and White** (no gray) (depending on your printer).

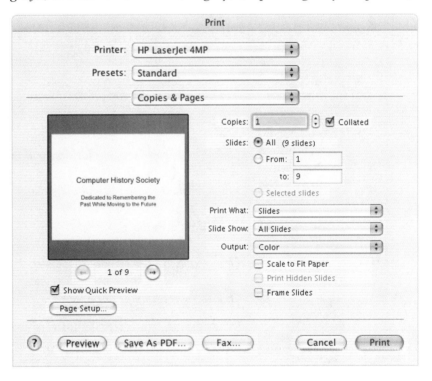

Scale to Fit Paper *changes size to accommodate paper size,* Print Hidden Slides *prints slides hidden from normal viewing, and* Frame Slides *puts border around slides.*

4 **Check printer's paper supply**

If you're printing overheads, you need to make sure transparency film is loaded in paper tray you're using.

5 **Click Print to start printing (or Cancel if you're not printing now)**

6 **Close file without saving changes when finished**

Print notes & handouts

You can also print the speaker notes and audience handouts you created earlier.

1 **Open Notes file**

2 **Choose general print options**

On **File** menu, choose **Print**.

In **Copies** text box, type number.

If you're printing several copies and want each complete copy separated from next one, click **Collated**.

In **Print range** area, select **All** or enter a range.

3 **Choose PowerPoint print options**

On pop-up menu to right of **Print What**, view options.

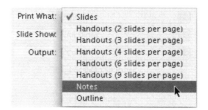

You must issue one print command for each type of output you want.

Choose **Notes**.

4 **Click Print to start printing (or Cancel if you're not printing now)**

5 **When finished, close file without saving changes**

6 **Open Handouts file**

7 **Choose general print options (see step 2)**

8 **Choose PowerPoint print options**

Do step 3, but on **Print What** pop-up menu, choose one of handouts options.

9 **Click Print to start printing (or Cancel if you're not printing now)**

10 **When finished, close file without saving changes**

Use template

Microsoft Office provides many fully designed presentations that you can use as the starting point for one of your own.

1 **View existing presentation templates**

On **File** menu, choose **Project Gallery**.

In **Groups** list, click ▶ to left of **Presentations**. Click **Content**.

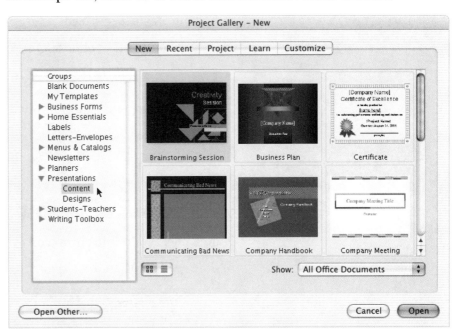

Scroll through table showing titles and designs of available presentations.

2 **Open new file based on presentation template**

Locate presentation you would like to use.

Click title or sample screen. Click **Open**.

New presentation opens with content and design coming from template.

3 **Explore new file**

Click each button at lower left of window to see different views.

On **View** menu, choose **Master**, then **Slide Master**.

Formatting on master gives consistent appearance to all slides. You could make changes here if you wanted to vary overall format.

On **Format** menu, choose **Slide Color Scheme**.

Dialog box shows current scheme and others you could use.

Click **Cancel**.

4 **Close file**

Do not save changes.

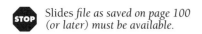

Save as Web page

You can save a Microsoft PowerPoint presentation as Web pages for displaying your presentation on the World Wide Web.

1 **Open Microsoft PowerPoint and** Slides *file*

2 **Save file as Web page and quit** PowerPoint

On **File** menu, choose **Save as Web Page**. Save file in your **My Files** folder with name `WebSlides.htm`.

On **PowerPoint** menu, choose **Quit PowerPoint**. If asked, don't save.

3 **View Web file and new folder**

On Finder's **File** menu, choose **New Finder Window**. Navigate to your **My Files** folder.

On **View** menu, choose **as Icons**. Locate both **WebSlides** icons.

Saving presentation as Web page creates file and supplemental files in folder.

4 **Open Web file in browser, and view slides**

Double-click **WebSlides.htm** icon.

File opens in Microsoft Explorer browser.

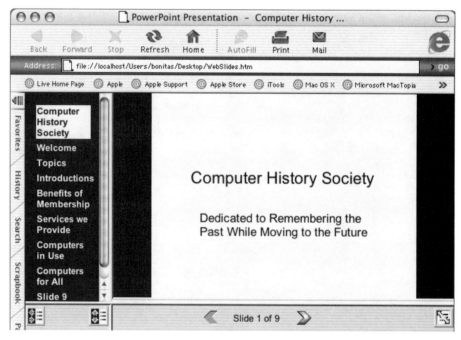

Click ▷ to move forward through slides. Click ◁ to move backward.

Tip

If you want to edit the Web page, you can open the file in PowerPoint and edit as a standard presentation. Save the file as a Web page again, and replace the original.

5 **End PowerPoint activities**

On **Explorer** menu, choose **Quit Explorer**.

If you're using floppy disk, eject it as shown on page 5, step 5.

On Apple menu, choose **Shut Down**.

Start Microsoft Excel

You are now ready to start the Microsoft Excel application to create spreadsheets and charts.

View
- ✓ Normal
- Page Layout
- Page Break Preview

- Toolbox
- Formatting Palette
- Toolbars ▶
- Ruler
- ✓ Formula Bar
- ✓ Status Bar

- Header and Footer...
- Comments

1 *Start computer and Excel*

Switch on computer (see page 2).

Do steps on page 7, but choosing **Microsoft Excel** now. Icon is .

2 *View desktop and document window for Microsoft Excel*

On **View** menu, make sure **Normal**, **Formula Bar**, and **Status Bar** are checked. See items in figure below.

If dotted vertical line appears (page break indicator), ignore for now.

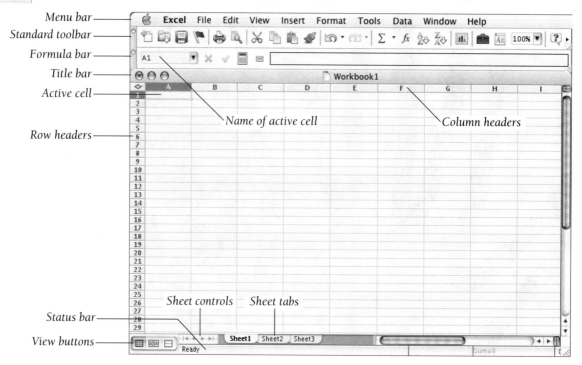

Menu bar — Standard toolbar — Formula bar — Title bar — Active cell — Name of active cell — Column headers — Row headers — Sheet controls — Sheet tabs — Status bar — View buttons

Place pointer on any icon on either bar at top to see name. *Do not click!*

3 *Notice thick border around cell A1*

> *Intersections of columns and rows form rectangles called "cells." One with border is "active" cell. This is where data will appear when you type.*

By the way

Microsoft Excel files are called workbooks. Each new workbook normally contains three blank worksheets. You'll usually use just one.

4 *Explore workbook*

To switch to different sheet, click its tab (at bottom of window) once.

> *Active worksheet tab is white; others are light gray.*

Notice sheet control buttons at bottom of window.

> *Buttons are for scrolling to any sheet tabs not visible. Currently you see all.*

Notice view buttons at lower left of window.

> *Buttons are for changing how worksheet appears.*

Click **Sheet1** to make worksheet 1 active.

Complete previous activity before going on.

Set preferences

User settings can affect the way Excel looks and works. You'll set the options and preferences expected in this book.

1 Disable AutoCorrect settings

On **Tools** menu, choose **AutoCorrect**.

Remove any check marks you see. Click **OK**.

2 Set preferences

On **Excel** menu, choose **Preferences**. Click **View** in left pane, and make options match figure below.

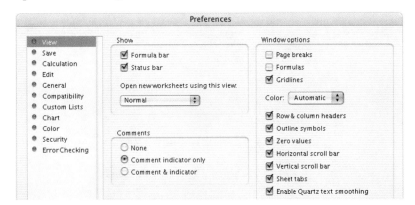

On **Edit** pane, make options match figure below.

On **General** pane, make options match figure below.

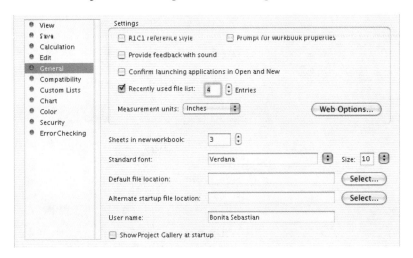

Click **OK** to approve all settings.

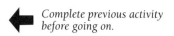
Explore worksheet

A worksheet is a set of cells arranged in rows and columns.
You'll learn how to navigate to and select cells.

1 **Select one cell**

Move pointer over worksheet. Notice shape: ✛ . Click pointer in any cell.

Active cell border moves to cell you selected.

Click cell A1.

2 **Notice active cell name at left of formula bar**

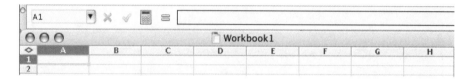

Name is column letter plus row number of active cell on worksheet.

Click another cell.

Notice that cell name changes in formula bar.

3 **Practice keyboard moves**

Tap (RETURN) to move *down* one cell. Tap (SHIFT)(RETURN) to move *up* one cell.

Tap (TAB) to move *right* one cell. Tap (SHIFT)(TAB) to move *left* one cell.

Tap →, ←, ↑, ↓ to move one cell in direction of arrow.

4 **Select range of cells (method 1)**

With pointer inside cell A1, press mouse button. Drag pointer to cell C3.

By the way

The column letter and row number headers of the selected cells are darkened.

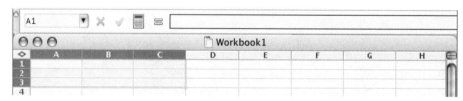

Rectangular range (multiple cells) is selected (highlighted). Notice that first cell remains white. This is active cell in range.

5 **Deselect range**

Click any cell on worksheet.

6 **Select range of cells (method 2)**

Click cell at upper left of range, hold down (SHIFT), and click lower-right cell.

7 **Select range of cells (method 3)**

Click cell at one corner of range.

With (SHIFT) held down, tap arrow keys to "paint" (or "unpaint") highlighting in direction of arrow.

> **A new worksheet must be open.**

Enter text

Entering data is usually the first step in creating a spreadsheet. You enter text by selecting a cell, then typing.

1 **Enter text in cell A1**

Click cell A1 if it's not already active.

Watch formula bar and cell as you type Computer Purchase Projections.

Use DELETE to erase typing errors.

Notice ✖ (cancel) and ✔ (enter) buttons on formula bar.

> *Entry is not complete yet.*

Tip

Remember that your entry is not complete until you click the enter button (or go to another cell). If some Excel commands don't seem to be working, look at the formula bar. If the cancel and enter buttons are not dimmed, it means you forgot to complete the entry.

---

2 **Accept entry in cell**

Click ✔ on formula bar.

> *Active cell stays A1. Although text appears to overlap cells B1 and C1, it's all in A1.*

3 **Begin entry; then change your mind**

With cell A1 still active, type Planned Purchases.

Click ✖ on formula bar, or tap ESC on keyboard.

> *Entry is canceled, and cell A1 is unchanged.*

Tip

Tapping TAB also completes data entry, but it makes the cell to the right become active.

---

4 **Select new cell, and enter text**

Click cell A3, and type IBM.

Tap RETURN on keyboard.

> *Text is entered, and active cell changes to A4, cell below entry.*

Type Dell. Tap RETURN to enter data and move to cell A5.

5 **Enter more data**

Type Appel (yes, it's misspelled). Tap RETURN to enter data.

> *Active cell should be A6.*

Type Acer.

Tap CONTROL RETURN to end data entry and leave cell active.

> CONTROL RETURN *is equivalent to clicking* ✔.

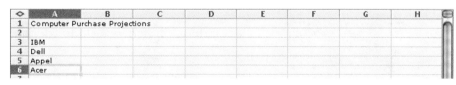

6 **Delete characters, and correct errors (method 1)**

Click cell with error to be corrected (A5).

In formula bar, click I-beam pointer just right of error (**el**).

Insertion point appears where you clicked.

Tap DELETE twice to erase error characters; then type le .

Tap CONTROL RETURN or click ✓ on formula bar to accept editing.

7 **Replace data already in cell**

Click cell A6.

Once cell is selected, just type new information.

Type Sonny and tap RETURN to accept change.

Sonny *replaces* Acer *in cell A6.*

8 **Delete characters, and correct errors (method 2)**

Sony *is spelled incorrectly.*

Double-click cell A6 in worksheet.

This time, insertion point appears in cell, not formula bar.

Position I-beam pointer just right of either **n**.

Tap DELETE to erase error.

Tap RETURN to accept change.

9 **Delete data in cell**

Click cell A1.

On **Edit** menu, choose **Clear**; on submenu, choose **All**.

You can also use DEL *for this if key is present on your keyboard.*

10 **Undo and redo previous change**

On **Edit** menu, choose **Undo Clear** (or tap ⌘ Z or click ↺ on standard toolbar).

On **Edit** menu, choose **Redo Clear** (or tap ⌘ Y or click ↻).

Text is cleared again.

Use any method to undo change once more.

Clear is undone, and text reappears in cell A1.

By the way

Notice that the Undo *command names the step you just did. You can also undo multiple actions by using the list on the undo tool on the standard toolbar.*

Complete previous activity
before going on.

Enter numbers & save

*As you'll soon see, the power of spreadsheets lies in their ability
to do calculations with numerical data.*

1 Enter numbers in column B

> *Column B will contain the quantity of computers to be purchased in the first
> month.*

Click cell B3.

Type 11 .

Tap RETURN .

> *Active cell is now B4.*

Type 10 and tap RETURN .

> *Active cell is now B5.*

Type 17 and tap RETURN .

> *Active cell is now B6.*

Type 15 and tap RETURN .

By the way
You can enter numbers by using the
keys at the top of the standard
keyboard or on the numeric keypad
on the right side of the keyboard.

2 Add more numbers in column C

Click cell C3.

Type 14 and tap RETURN . Type 9 and tap RETURN .

> *If List Wizard appears, click* No.

Type 12 and tap RETURN . Type 20 and tap RETURN .

3 Enter numbers in column D

Enter these numbers in column D: 9 , 12 , 16 , 14 .

> *Spreadsheet should look like figure below.*

	A	B	C	D	E	F	G	H
1	Computer Purchase Projections							
2								
3	IBM	11	14	9				
4	Dell	10	9	12				
5	Apple	17	12	16				
6	Sony	15	20	14				
7								

4 Save workbook file

If you're using floppy disk, make sure it's inserted now.

On **File** menu, choose **Save** (or click 💾 on standard toolbar).

Type Plans as name of file. Leave extension as **.xls**.

Navigate to your **My Files** folder (see page 19, step 3, for details).

Name of saved document ——
Place to save it ——

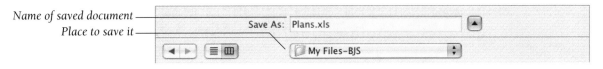

Click **Save.**

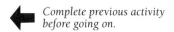

*Complete previous activity
before going on.*

Select cells

*Many commands affect only the cells that you select before
giving the command. Selected cells are highlighted.*

1 **Select cells with data for computers**

Click cell A3.

Hold SHIFT down, then click cell D6.

> *Shift-clicking extends selection. A3 remains active cell.*

2 **Move active cell through selected block**

Watch active cell as you tap TAB repeatedly. Try same with RETURN.

> *This is convenient when entering data in table.*

3 **Select one whole column**

Put pointer in ⌐ A ⌐ (header for column A). Click down-arrow pointer.

> *Whole column is highlighted. First cell in column is active cell.*

4 **Select several whole columns**

With pointer inside column B header, press mouse button, and drag to
right to highlight columns C and D.

At left of first selected column, notice box indicating number of columns
selected. Release mouse button.

> *All cells are highlighted. Different highlighting (white) shows B1 is active.*

5 **Select one row, then several rows**

Click right-arrow pointer in ⌐3→⌐ (header for row 3).

> *Whole row is highlighted.*

Press inside row 3 header (*not* line between row headers), and drag down
to highlight rows 4, 5, and 6. Notice which cell is active.

6 **Select whole spreadsheet**

Click ⌐◇⌐ (select all) button above row 1 and to left of column A.

By the way

*The pointer changes to a diagonal
arrow when in the select all box.
The arrow reminds you that all
cells in the worksheet will be
selected.*

7 **Select separated rows**

Click header for row 1.

Hold down ⌘, and click headers for rows 4 and 6. Notice active cell.

> ⌘ *lets you add any cells you want to current selection.*

Click any cell to deselect block.

8 **Close workbook**

On **File** menu, choose **Close**. If asked, do not save changes.

Plans *file as saved on page 135 must be available.*

Print workbook

You can print a selected block of cells, a single sheet, or all sheets in a workbook.

1 **Open Plans workbook file from your My Files folder**

For reminder of steps for opening files, see page 21.

2 **View page breaks**

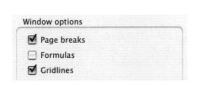

On **Excel** menu, choose **Preferences**. On **View** page of dialog box, under **Window options**, select **Page breaks**. Click **OK**.

On toolbar's zoom pop-up menu, choose **75%**.

Dashed lines mark boundaries of print areas on pages.

3 **Switch to page layout view and back**

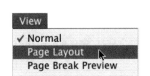

On **View** menu, choose **Page Layout**. Notice page margins.

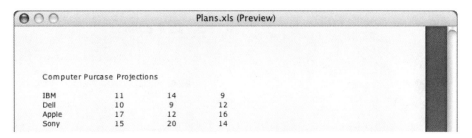

Return to normal view.

4 **Preview printing**

On standard toolbar, choose 🔍 (print preview).

Preview has only one page. Blank pages won't be printed.

On preview toolbar, click Close.

5 **Select block of cells to print (method 1)**

Select cell range A3:D6 (table only).

On **File** menu, choose **Print Area**, then **Set Print Area**.

Dashed lines now appear only around area you selected.

On standard toolbar, choose 🔍 again to see results. Then close preview.

6 *Select block of cells to print (method 2)*

Click any cell to deselect block of cells now highlighted.

On **View** menu, choose **Page Break Preview**. Click **OK** if dialog box like one at left appears.

> *Thick blue borders show current page breaks. You can move them.*

Put pointer on upper blue border. Notice pointer shape: ⟦⟧ .

Drag border up to top of worksheet.

Return to normal view. Notice dashed borders showing print area now.

7 *Clear selected print area*

On **File** menu, choose **Print Area**, then **Clear Print Area**.

> *Dashed lines return to showing automatic page breaks.*

8 *Insert page break, then remove it*

Click header for row 5. On **Insert** menu, choose **Page Break**.

> *Dashed line shows break above selected row.*

Preview printed pages. Look at both pages. Then close preview.

With row 5 still selected, choose **Remove Page Break** on **Insert** menu.

9 *Set up page for printing*

On **View** menu, choose **Formatting Palette** (or click [A≣] on standard toolbar).

Notice **Page Setup** options on **Formatting Palette**.

> *Same options can be controlled by* Page Setup *command on* File *menu.*

Watch dashed lines on worksheet as you click [Landscape] , then [Portrait] .

Look at **Print Scaling** options.

> *They're useful when working with large spreadsheets.*

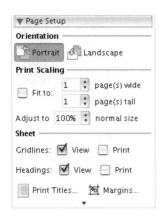

Look at **Sheet** options. Watch worksheet as you click **View** check boxes for **Gridlines** and for **Headings**. Click same check boxes again.

> *Check boxes in* Print *dialog box let you control printing of same features.*

Click [Margins...] to open **Page Setup** dialog box at **Margins** page.

> *You can change margins of all pages and center output between margins.*

If necessary, drag **Formatting Palette** aside.

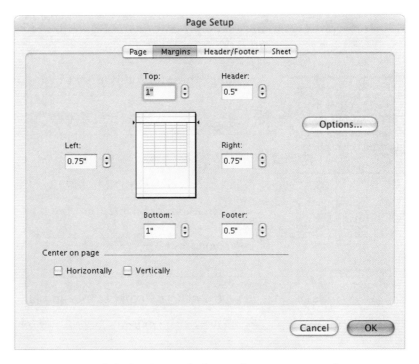

In bar at top of dialog box, click **Header/Footer**. Look at items on pop-up menus.

You can choose among standard items or create your own.

Click **Cancel** to leave options unchanged.

10 *Close Formatting Palette*

At upper left of palette, click 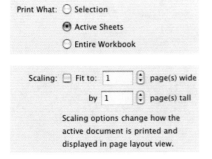 to close it.

You won't need palette again until page 147.

11 *Print workbook*

Make sure printer is connected and switched on.

On **File** menu, choose **Print**. Notice many familiar features.

Printing works same way in most applications, but new features appear here.

Notice new **Print What** options.

Selection *lets you print just selected cells without having to set print area.* *Active Sheets* *means sheet you're working on (and any others you've selected by shift-clicking sheet tabs).* Entire workbook *means all sheets.*

Notice new **Scaling** options.

These are same as ones on Page Setup *pane of* Formatting Palette.

When ready, click **Print** button (or **Cancel** if you're not ready to print).

12 *Close document window without saving changes*

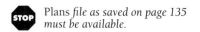
Explore workbooks

You can rename a sheet in a workbook, add and delete sheets, and change sheet order.

1 **Open Plans workbook file from your My Files folder**

2 **Select sheets**

Notice three tabs at bottom of window and dimmed arrow buttons to left.

By the way

The set of arrow buttons becomes active when the worksheet tabs are too big or too numerous to fit in the space to the right. You can then use the buttons to move tabs into view.

Click **Sheet2** tab. Notice empty worksheet (in page layout view).

Click **Sheet1** tab; then hold down ⌘, and click **Sheet3**.

Both tabs are white, showing they are selected (possibly for printing).

3 **Rename sheet**

Double-click **Sheet1** text on tab.

By the way

You can use up to 31 characters for a sheet name.

Type 1st Qtr Projections and tap RETURN.

New name appears on tab, and tab widens to fit text.

4 **Add, move, and delete worksheets**

Select second worksheet.

On **Insert** menu, choose **Worksheet**.

New worksheet, named Sheet4, is inserted just before selected sheet.

Press first tab, and drag to move small triangle just right of **Sheet4** tab.

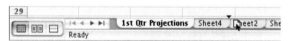

Worksheet and contents move after Sheet 4.

Select **Sheet4** worksheet. On **Edit** menu, choose **Delete Sheet**.

Message means you can't undo deletion!

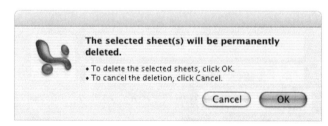

Click **OK**.

5 **Close workbook file without saving changes**

Original sheet names and order remain unchanged.

Enter simple formulas

You can enter simple formulas in spreadsheets by using the keyboard or mouse.

1 **Create new workbook file**

Click 🗋 (new) on standard toolbar.

Change view to normal.

2 **Enter numbers to create following worksheet (enlarged for legibility)**

◇	A	B	C	D	E
1					
2					
3	123	321	741	1471	
4	456	654	852	2582	
5	789	987	963	3693	
6					

3 **Save workbook**

On **File** menu, choose **Save**.

Save in your **My Files** folder with name **Numprac**.

4 **Enter formula (method 1)**

Use arrow keys to select cell A7.

Type = .

> *Formulas always begin with =.*

Type a3+a4 .

> *You don't have to type capital letters for cell names.*

Tap ⎣CONTROL⎦⎣RETURN⎦.

5 **Observe formula and results**

Look at formula bar and worksheet cell A7.

> *Formula bar shows what was entered into file for cell A7 (=A3+A4). Cell A7 on worksheet shows result (579).*

Click outside cell A7.

> *Result stays on worksheet, but formula is not in formula bar now.*

Click cell A7 to see formula again.

6 **Enter formula (method 2)**

Click cell B7 to select it as place for formula. Click ▤ (edit formula).

Click cell B3, then B4. Click **OK** in dialog box that appeared under formula.

> *Excel automatically puts + before B4 in formula. (If you wanted something else, you'd have to type it before clicking B4.)*

Click ✔ to accept entry.

7 **Observe results**

Formula bar should contain =B3+B4. Cell B7 should display 975.

8 **Enter subtraction formula (method 3)**

Click cell B8. Type = .

Watch formula bar as you tap ⬆ to select cell B7.

Type - .

Tap ⬆ and ⬅ to select cell A7.

Tap CONTROL RETURN . Check formula and result.

Formula should read =B7–A7. Result in cell B8 should be 396.

9 **Enter multiplication formula**

Select cell B10.

Use any method to enter formula =B7*B8 .

For asterisk (*), which stands for multiplication sign, tap SHIFT 8 or use key on numeric keypad.

Click ✔ .

Check formula and result.

Result in cell B10 should be 386100.

10 **Enter division formula**

Select cell B12.

Use any method to enter formula =B7/A7 .

Slash (/) is on both main keyboard and numeric keypad.

Click ✔ . Check formula and result.

Result in cell B12 should be 1.68393782.

11 **Enter more complex formula**

Select cell B14.

Use any method to enter formula =A3+A4+B3+B4 .

Click ✔ .

Check formula and result.

Result in cell B14 should be 1554.

12 **Close workbook without saving changes**

On **File** menu, choose **Close**.

Click **Don't Save** in message box when asked whether to save changes.

Tip

Be careful about arrow keys. Normally, they move the selection from one cell to another. But when you are entering a formula, an arrow key enters a cell name. If that happens by accident, delete the name, and continue.

STOP Plans *file as saved on page 135 must be available.*

1 Open Plans workbook file

If using floppy disk, make sure it's in drive.

On **File** menu, choose **Open**.

Use steps on page 21 to navigate to your **My Files** folder.

In list of files, double-click **Plans**.

2 Enter formula with function (method 1)

Select cell B8, where result of formula will appear.

Type =sum(b3:b6) and tap [CONTROL] [RETURN].

> *Formula uses SUM function to add numbers in cell range B3:B6. (You don't have to use capital letters when typing function names or cell names.)*

Check formula and result.

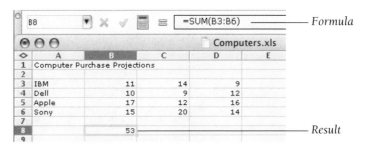

3 Enter formula with function (method 2)

Click cell C8, where result of second formula will appear. Type =sum(.

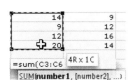

Put pointer in cell C3. Press and drag down to cell C6. Release mouse button.

> *When you're entering formulas, dragging through cells enters cell range.*

Click ✓. Notice that Excel enters closing parenthesis for you.

Check formula and result.

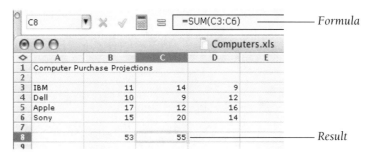

4 Delete both formulas

Highlight cells B8 and C8.

On **Edit** menu, choose **Clear**, then **All** (or tap [DEL]).

5   *Enter formula with function (method 3)*

Click cell B8, where result of formula will appear.

On standard toolbar, click Σ (AutoSum).

> *Formula =SUM(B3:B7) appears in formula bar (and on worksheet) with "marching ants" marking cell range, which includes blank cell B7.*

Click ✔. Notice tiny comment triangle and nearby button:

> *Result is same as in step 2. What's up?*

Click ⚠ (error button) to see message and options.

> *You're warned that formula refers to empty cell. That won't affect sum.*

On pop-up menu, choose **Ignore Error**.

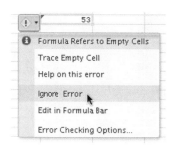

6   *Use AutoSum button again*

Click cell C8, where result will appear.

On standard toolbar, click Σ again. Check formula.

> *Formula =SUM(C3:C7) appears.*

Click ✔. Ignore "error" as above. Check result.

> *Result is same as in step 3.*

7   *Use AutoSum once more*

Click cell D8, where result will appear. On standard toolbar, click Σ again.

Check formula.

> *Oops! Formula is not correct: =SUM(B8:C8). AutoSum picks closest data range, and in this case that is wrong. Cell range is already highlighted in formula, so it's easy to change.*

On worksheet, press and drag from cell D3 down to cell D7.

> *Notice that formula in formula bar (and on worksheet) changes. Formula should be =SUM(D3:D7).*

Click ✔. Ignore "error" as above. Check result.

> *Correct sum is 51.*

8   *Enter label for sums*

Click cell A8. Type Total and tap [RETURN].

9   *Save workbook file*

On **File** menu, choose **Save**.

> *No dialog box appears. Edited version of* Plans *replaces previously saved version.*

Tip

For automatic entry of other common functions, click the arrow to the right of the AutoSum button to see a pop-up menu of names.

By the way

You can also edit the formula by typing in the correct range.

Copy formula (relative)

Microsoft Excel allows you to copy formulas from one cell to many other cells quickly and easily.

1 *Enter title for totals in column E*

Click cell E2. Type `Totals by Computer` and tap `RETURN`.

2 *Enter another addition formula using AutoSum*

With cell E3 active, click Σ (AutoSum) on standard toolbar. Verify formula.

Formula should be =SUM(B3:D3).

Click ✔ to accept formula. Check that result on worksheet is **34**.

3 *Copy formula to other cells (method 1)*

Position pointer over handle (small square in lower-right corner of active cell border).

Pointer changes shape when at handle. (If handle is not present, set Edit preferences as shown on page 131, step 2.)

2				Totals by Computer	
3	IBM	11	14	9	34
4	Dell	10	9	12	

Tip

The pointer must be in a precise location for the handle to work. Watch for the proper pointer shape.

Press and drag handle down to cell E6.

Notice outline showing range where data is to be copied.

Release mouse button.

Formula is copied down. You can also copy up, copy left, and copy right. Direction depends on where you drag handle.

◇	A	B	C	D	E	F	G	H	
1	Computer Purchase Projections								
2					Totals by Computer				
3	IBM	11	14	9	34				
4	Dell	10	9	12	31				
5	Apple	17	12	16	45				
6	Sony	15	20	14	49				

Click each cell containing copied formula. Look at formula bar.

Cell names have changed from original (B3:D3) to be "relative" to location of copy of formula. For example, if copy is in row 4, range is B4:D4.

By the way

You must use the copy-and-paste method when the cell where you want the copy is not next to the cell with the original.

4 *Copy and paste formula (method 2)*

Click cell D8. Notice formula in formula bar. On **Edit** menu, choose **Copy** (or click 🗐 on standard toolbar).

Click cell E8. On **Edit** menu, choose **Paste** (or click 🗐 on toolbar). Ignore "error."

Cell D8 keeps dashed outline, showing that you can paste again.

Verify that result is **159** and that cell names have changed in copy of formula so that numbers in column E are summed.

5 *Save changed workbook file*

On **File** menu, choose **Save**.

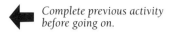
Complete previous activity before going on.

Enter data series

Excel makes it easy to enter standard data series, such as days of the week, months, quarters, or years.

1 **Enter first item in series**

Click cell B2. Type `January` and tap CONTROL RETURN.

2 **Create series of months**

Carefully press handle (at lower right), and drag to surround range B2 through D2. Notice box below pointer.

◇	A	B	C	D
1	Computer Purchase Projections			
2		January		⌐⌐T
3	IBM	11	14	March
4	Dell	10	9	

Release mouse button.

Cell C2 now contains February, *and D2 contains* March.

By the way

This method also works with days of the week. If you begin the series with an abbreviation, such as Jan *or* Wed, *or if you use all capital letters, the rest of the series follows your example.*

3 **Save changed workbook file**

4 **Try another data series**

Click cell B10. Type `2004` and click ✓.

Press and drag handle to surround range B10 through D10.

Release mouse button. Look at cells C10 and D10.

Both contain 2004. Dragging handle this time simply copied number. Excel had no formula or list to use.

5 **Use Fill Series command to create series of years**

Make sure cells B10 through D10 are still selected.

On **Edit** menu, choose **Fill**; on submenu, choose **Series**.

Type of series is Linear *and Step value is* 1. *That's what you want now.*

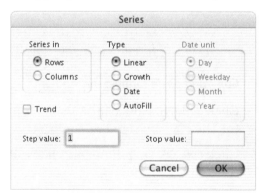

Click **OK**.

Cell C10 now contains 2005, and D10 contains 2006.

Tip

You can also add your own series to the built-in lists. On the Excel *menu, choose* Preferences. *Click* Custom Lists, *and use the* Add *button to add your own list.*

6 **Close workbook file without saving changes**

On **File** menu, choose **Close**. Click **Don't Save** in dialog box.

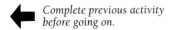

Complete previous activity before going on.

Copy formula (absolute)

Relative change of cell names is normally what you want in a copy of a formula—but not always. Here's an example.

1 **Open Plans workbook file from your My Files folder**

2 **Create new column title**

Click cell F2. Type `Percent of Total` and tap RETURN. (If asked about List Manager, click **No**.)

> *Column F will show each computer's projected purchase as percentage of grand total (159 in cell E8).*

By the way

When text is entered in cell F2, text in E2 appears truncated. It's still there but no longer displayed. You'll fix this later.

3 **Calculate and display percentages**

On standard toolbar, click 🅰 to open **Formatting Palette**.

With cell F3 active, use any method to enter formula `=E3/E8`.

> *Result is 0.21383648. You want this shown as percentage.*

Make sure cell F3 is selected.

In **Number** pane of **Formatting Palette**, choose **Percentage**, on **Format** pop-up menu.

In same pane, click ⬇︎ (decrease decimal) twice.

> *Same number now appears as 21%. (You'll learn more about formatting numbers on page 160.)*

4 **Copy formula down column**

Press and drag cell F3 handle down to cell F6. Release mouse button.

> *Oops! Something is wrong! Instead of percentages, #DIV/0 appears.*

Click cell F4. Move pointer over ⓘ (error button) to left of cell F4.

2		January	February	March		Totals by Cor	Percent of Total	
3	IBM	11	14	9		34	21%	
4	Dell	10	9	12	ⓘ ▾		#DIV/0!	
5	Apple	17	12	16			#DIV/0!	
6	Sony	15	20	14		The formula or function used is dividing by	
7						zero or empty cells.	

> *#DIV/0 in cell means formula is trying to divide number by zero.*

5 **View formulas in cells on worksheet**

Tap CONTROL `~`. Scroll so columns E and F are both in view.

> `~` *is at left of row of number keys on main keyboard.* CONTROL `~` *switches between view of results and view of formulas in cells.*

If necessary, scroll so columns E and F are both in view.

By the way

CONTROL `~` *is a shortcut for an option you can also set by choosing* Preferences *on the* Excel *menu, clicking* View, *then clicking the* Formulas *check box.*

2	February	March	Totals by Computer	Percent of Total
3	14	9	=SUM(B3:D3)	=E3/E8
4	9	12	=SUM(B4:D4) ⓘ	=E4/E9
5	12	16	=SUM(B5:D5)	=E5/E10
6	20	14	=SUM(B6:D6)	=E6/E11
7				
8	=SUM(C3:C7)	=SUM(D3:D7)	=SUM(E3:E7)	
9				

6   *View formulas causing errors*

Look at formula in cell F4. Notice green color of border of empty cell E9.

> *Formula is =E4/E9. There is no number in cell E9.*

Look at formulas in cells F5 and F6.

> *You wanted E3 to change relative to new location, but E8 needs to remain constant in each copy so formulas all refer to grand total.*

7   *Make divisor stay same in copies*

Double-click cell F3.

Put insertion point between **E** and **8**.

Type **$** and click ☑.

> *Formula should be =E3/E$8. Dollar sign makes 8 absolute. It won't change in copies. The 3 in E3 is still relative. It will change in copies in other rows.*

Press and drag handle again to surround range F3:F6.

Release mouse button, and look at copies this time.

> *The 8 in E8 remains constant ("absolute") in all copies of formula.*

By the way

Cell names in formulas are often called "references" because they refer to the data in the cell. A dollar sign before a row letter or a column number makes it an "absolute reference."

2	February	March	Totals by Computer	Percent of Total
3	14	9	=SUM(B3:D3)	=E3/E$8
4	9	12	=SUM(B4:D4)	=E4/E$8
5	12	16	=SUM(B5:D5)	=E5/E$8
6	20	14	=SUM(B6:D6)	=E6/E$8
7				
8	=SUM(C3:C7)	=SUM(D3:D7)	=SUM(E3:E7)	

8   *View results in worksheet cells*

Tap ⎡CONTROL ˜⎤ again to see results of formulas.

Scroll so that column A is back in view.

2		January	February	March	Totals by Co	Percent of Total		
3	IBM	11	14	9	34	21%		
4	Dell	10	9	12	31	19%		
5	Apple	17	12	16	45	28%		
6	Sony	15	20	14	49	31%		
7								
8	Total	53	55	51	159			
9								

> *Percentages appear correctly with new formulas.*

By the way

Percentages you see on the worksheet are rounded off, so they may not appear to add up to 100%. However, step 9 shows that the actual, unrounded percentages do add up to 100%.

9   *Verify correctness of formula, then clear cell*

Click cell F7. On formula bar, click **Σ** (AutoSum). Click ☑.

> *Result should be 100%. Same formatting (percentage with no decimal places) is automatically applied to cell with formula.*

On **Edit** menu, choose **Clear**, then **All** (or tap ⎡DEL⎤).

> *All option erases both contents and applied formats of cell.*

10   *Save changed workbook*

Complete previous activity before going on.

Insert function

If you forget the exact name of a function, you can find it on a list and paste it directly into a formula.

1 *Add another text label to worksheet*

Click cell A9. Type `Average` and tap `TAB`.

2 *Enter formula in cell to right of label*

In cell B9, type `=` to begin formula.

> *This is cell where average projections for January will appear.*

On **Insert** menu, choose **Function** (or click `fx` on standard toolbar).

> *Paste Function dialog box appears. It lists all available functions.*

In **Function category** list, choose **Statistical**.

> *Functions for working with lists of numbers are grouped here.*

In **Function name** list, click **AVERAGE**.

> *Description of function appears at bottom of dialog box.*

By the way

The few functions you'll use in this activity are also available on the AutoSum pop-up menu on the toolbar. You'll need the methods learned here for all the rest.

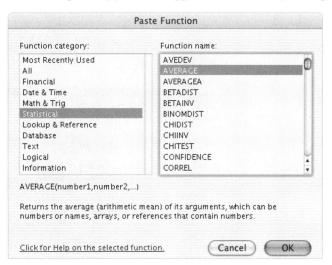

Click **OK** button.

> *New window (without title bar) appears under formula bar.*

In **Number1** text box, change range to **B3:B6** (January cells to be averaged).

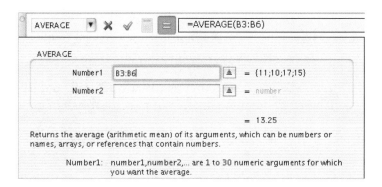

Click **OK**.

> *Formula is inserted, and result (13.25) appears on worksheet.*

3 *Copy formula to other months and total*

Press cell B9 handle carefully, and drag to surround range B9:E9. Release mouse button.

Verify that results are **13.75**, **12.75**, and **39.75** and that cell names in formulas have changed to be relative to new locations of copies.

4 *Add another label to worksheet*

Click cell A10.

Type Maximum and tap (TAB).

5 *Add MAX function*

With cell B10 active, click 𝑓𝑥 (paste function) on standard toolbar.

> *Clicking button automatically puts = in formula bar.*

In **Function category** list, make sure **Statistical** is selected.

In **Function name** list, choose **MAX** (maximum).

Click **OK** button.

Drag dialog box down so that you can see cells with numbers.

Highlight range B3:B6 to put cell range in formula. Tap (RETURN).

> *Formula is inserted, and result (17) appears on worksheet.*

Copy formula to range C10:E10.

Verify that results are **20**, **16**, and **49** and that cell addresses have changed to be relative to new locations of copies.

6 *Add another function in next row*

Type Minimum label in cell A11. Tap (TAB).

With cell B11 active, click 𝑓𝑥 again.

In **Function category** list, make sure **Statistical** is selected.

In **Function name** list, choose **MIN** (minimum).

Use method in step 5 to add range B3:B6.

Copy formula to range C11:E11.

Verify that results are **10**, **9**, **9**, and **31** and that cell addresses have changed to be relative to new locations of copies.

7 *Save and close changed workbook file*

On **File** menu, choose **Save**.

On **File** menu, choose **Close**.

Numprac file as saved on page 141 must be available.

Paste special

You can paste copied data using many special formats. Here you will practice a few of them.

1 **Open Numprac workbook file from your My Files folder**

2 **Use formula to add multiple columns of numbers**

Select range A6:D6. On standard toolbar, click Σ . View results.

Formulas to sum numbers above selected range are automatically entered.

3 **Copy cells with formulas**

With range A6:D6 still selected, on **Edit** menu, choose **Copy**.

4 **Paste values only**

Click cell A8. On **Edit** menu, choose **Paste Special**.

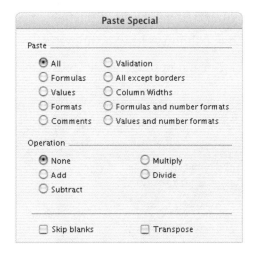

Click **Values**; click **OK**. Tap ESC to clear clipboard. View results.

Result of formula (value) is pasted, not formula.

5 **Transpose data (switch data in rows to columns, and vice versa)**

Select range A3:D5. On **Edit** menu, choose **Copy**.

11	123	456	789
12	321	654	987
13	741	852	963
14	1471	2582	3693

Click cell A11. On **Edit** menu, choose **Paste Special**. At lower right, click **Transpose**; click **OK**. Tap ESC to clear clipboard. View results.

6 **Add values (add copied data to data in paste range)**

Select range A3:D3. On **Edit** menu, choose **Copy**.

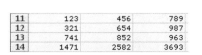

Click cell A4. On **Edit** menu, choose **Paste Special**.

Click **Add**; click **OK**. Tap ESC to clear clipboard. View results.

Four selected numbers in row 3 were added to ones already in row 4.

Look at formula bar for cell A4.

No formula is involved. Addition happened when you pasted.

7 **Close Numprac workbook without saving changes**

Format text

After entering data, you may wish to format text to emphasize and clarify. You can use menu commands or toolbar buttons.

1 **Open Plans workbook file from your My Files folder**

2 **Add bold style to labels (method 1)**

If necessary, click ⌧ to see **Formatting Palette**.

Highlight range A1:F2 (title in row 1 and column labels in row 2).

In **Font** pane of **Formatting Palette**, click **B** (bold).

> *Text in highlighted cells is now bold. Bold tool is darkened.*

> **By the way**
>
> *Not all text in a cell must be formatted the same way. To make some characters bold, for example, click the cell with the text, go to the formula bar, and highlight just the characters you want to be bold. Then apply bold format.*

3 **Remove bold from one cell**

Click cell A1. Click **B** (now darkened).

4 **Add bold style to labels (method 2)**

Click column A header (above cell A1) to select whole column.

On **Format** menu, choose **Cells**. Click **Font** in bar at top of dialog box.

> **By the way**
>
> *As you can see, the Format Cells dialog box lets you apply many different formats to the data in a cell. You'll use more of them soon.*

On **Font Style** list, click **Bold**. Click **OK**.

5 **Add bold style to labels (method 3)**

Click any cell with bold text.

On standard toolbar, click 🖌 (format painter).

Click header for row 8 (row of totals).

> *Format painter copies all formats from original cell (or block of cells), and "paints" them in whatever other cells you select.*

6 **Add italic to bold**

Select cells A3 through A6. In **Font** pane on **Formatting Palette**, click *I* (italic).

7 **Save changed workbook file**

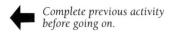

Complete previous activity before going on.

Change fonts & sizes

Text can appear in many different fonts and sizes. Each font specifies the shapes of letters, numbers, and symbols.

1 **Choose cell to apply format change**

Click cell A1.

> *Notice that text flows into cells B1 and C1 but is actually contained in cell A1 (check formula bar). Overflow appears when neighbor cell is empty.*

2 **Check current font and size**

In **Font** area of **Formatting Palette**, notice **Verdana** font in size **10**.

> *These are defaults you set earlier for new worksheets.*

On **Formatting Palette**, click ▼ to see **Name** pop-up menu.

> *Your menu of fonts may be different from list below.*

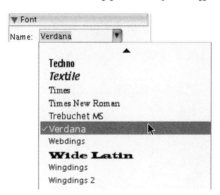

3 **Change font and size**

On **Name** pop-up menu, scroll down, and choose **Times**.

> *Command affects only text in selected cell.*

In **Font** pane on **Formatting Palette**, click ▼ to see **Size** pop-up menu.

On Size menu, choose **14**. Notice that row height adjusts to font size.

4 **Change font size of another range**

Highlight cells in range A8:E8.

> *This is row of totals.*

On Size pop-up menu, click **12**.

5 **Save changed workbook file**

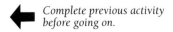 *Complete previous activity before going on.*

Change text alignment

Text can be aligned at left, right, or center within a cell. It can also be centered over a range of cells.

---

1 *Align data within cells (method 1)*

Highlight range B2:F2 (column labels you entered on pages 146 and 147).

In **Alignment and Spacing** pane of **Formatting Palette**, locate four horizontal alignment tools.

Click ▤ (align center). Notice centered text in selected cells.

Select range A8:A11 (function labels you entered on page 149).

On **Formatting Palette**, click ▤ (align right).

2 *Align data within cells (method 2)*

Highlight range B3:F11 (cells with numbers).

On **Format** menu, choose **Cells**. Click **Alignment** in bar at top.

> *Standard alignment settings and many other options are available.*

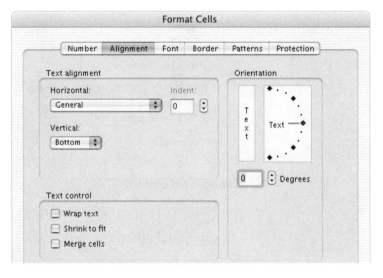

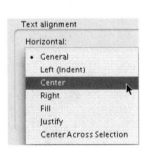

On **Horizontal** pop-up menu, choose **Center**. Click **OK**.

3 *Center title on selected columns*

Select range A1:F1. On **Format** menu, choose **Cells**.

If necessary, click **Alignment** in bar at top.

On **Horizontal** pop-up menu, choose **Center**. In **Text control** area, click **Merge cells** check box. Click **OK**.

> *Cells are merged into one large cell (named A1) with centered text.*

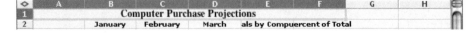

4 *Save changed workbook file*

STOP Plans *file as saved on page 148 (or later) must be open.*

Set column width & row height

You can easily change column widths and row heights, either one at a time or as a group.

1 *Change column width (method 1)*

Position pointer on right border of column F header.

When pointer changes shape, you can change width of column F.

You could drag left or right to change width. Here's a better way.

Double-click while pointer has above shape.

Width automatically adjusts to widest entry in column F.

Repeat above steps to adjust columns A and E.

2 *Change column width (method 2)*

Highlight any block of cells in columns B, C, and D.

On **Format** menu, choose **Column**, then **Width**.

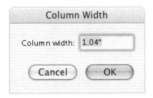

Type 1 and click **OK**.

Widths of all cells in all three columns are changed.

3 *Change row height (method 1)*

Carefully put pointer on bottom border of header for row 7 (blank row).

When pointer changes shape, you can change height of row above it.

Notice height in text box as you press mouse button.

First number is in points (72 points equal 1 inch).

6 Height: 13.00 (0.18 inches)	20	14	49	31%	
8 Total	53	55	51	159	

Press and drag up to adjust height to **7.00** (points).

Height indicator in text box shows change as you make it.

If you drag too far, drag back down again.

4 *Change row height (method 2)*

Highlight any block of cells in rows 2 through 6.

On **Format** menu, choose **Row**; on submenu, choose **Height**.

Notice that units are inches only. Type .2 and click **OK**.

5 *Save changed workbook file*

By the way

Another way to make a long label fit in a column is to make its text "wrap" inside its cell. The width of the column stays the same, and the height of the row expands to allow room for the wrapped text. To wrap text, open the Format Cells dialog box (see figure on page 154), and click the Wrap text check box toward the bottom.

Row Height

Row height: 0.18"

Cancel   OK

STOP Plans *file as saved on page 148 (or later) must be open.*

Insert & delete cells

You can insert blocks of new cells, including whole rows and columns. You can also delete existing cells.

1 Insert whole column of new cells

Click any cell in column B (except merged cell in row 1, if you did activity on page 154).

On **Insert** menu, choose **Columns**.

Empty cells are inserted in column B, pushing old columns to right.

Notice green comment triangles on cells at right. Click any such cell, and put pointer on [!] (error button) that appears.

Empty cell is one in new column. It won't affect sum. You can ignore message.

2 Insert whole row

Click any cell in row 6. On **Insert** menu, choose **Rows**. Ignore "errors."

Empty cells are inserted in row 6, pushing old rows down.

3 Insert multiple rows

Press and drag through headers to highlight rows 2 and 3.

Excel will insert as many rows as you select.

On **Insert** menu, choose **Rows**.

Two new rows of empty cells are inserted.

Click cell A2. Type `format test` and click ✓.

Text is bold, large, and centered in cell. New cell A2 got its formats from cell A1. Each inserted cell inherits format from cell above (or cell at left if column of cells is inserted).

4 Delete all cells in row

Click in header to highlight row 2. On **Edit** menu, choose **Delete**.

5 Insert rectangular block of new cells

Highlight cells in range B4:C6. On **Insert** menu, choose **Cells**.

Dialog box asks how to shift existing cells to make room for block.

By the way
You can also highlight and delete any block of cells. After choosing Delete on the Edit menu, you're asked how to move existing cells into the empty space after the block is removed. Notice this difference between deleting a cell and deleting the data in a cell. If you delete only the data (by choosing Clear on the Edit menu), other cells don't shift.

Click **Shift cells down**. Click **OK** to see effect.

6 Close Plans workbook file without saving changes

Hide gridlines & add borders

You can hide the gray gridlines and add custom borders to cells and ranges. The Borders palette makes adding borders easy.

1 **Open Plans workbook file from your My Files folder**

2 **Follow directions in this activity and next one to duplicate figure below**

◇	A	B	C	D	E	F	G	H
1			Computer Purchase Projections					
2		January	February	March	Totals by Computer	Percent of Total		
3	IBM	11	14	9	34	21%		
4	Dell	10	9	12	31	19%		
5	Apple	17	12	16	45	28%		
6	Sony	15	20	14	49	31%		
8	Total	53	55	51	159			
9	Average	13.25	13.75	12.75	39.75			
10	Maximum	17	20	16	49			
11	Minimum	10	9	9	31			

By the way

If you have not done all the previous activities, some of the contents and text formats in the figure may be missing.

3 **Hide gridlines**

On **Excel** menu, choose **Preferences**. In left pane, click **View**.

Under **Window options**, click to remove mark from **Gridlines** check box.

Tip

Suppressing the display of the default gridlines makes it easier to see borders you add. Default gridlines can be printed with a worksheet, but you get either all or none of them. Adding borders gives you more control.

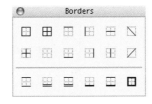

Click **OK**.

Standard gridlines no longer appear. You can add your own borders.

4 **View Border palette in front of worksheet**

On **Formatting Palette**, click **Borders and Shading**.

By the way

Many items on the Formatting Palette have "tear-off menus" that become palettes of their own.

Click ⊞ ▾ (border type) to see pop-up menu.

Click double bar at top of pop-up menu to tear off menu as **Borders** palette.

Tip

Each icon on the Borders palette shows where a border line will be added to selected cells and what type of border will appear.

5 **Add outline border to whole data area**

Highlight range A2:F11.

On **Borders** palette, click ▣ (thick box border).

Click any cell to deselect range and see result (thick borders around data area).

6 **Add bottom border (method 1)**

Highlight range A6:F6.

On **Borders** palette, click ⊡ (bottom border).

7 *Add bottom border (method 2)*

Highlight range B8:E8.

On **Format** menu, choose **Cells**; then click **Border** in bar at top.

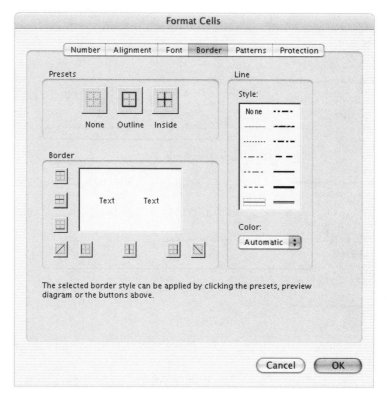

In **Style** list, click double line (last style in second column).

In **Border** area, click ▥ (bottom border). Click **OK**.

8 *Add interior vertical borders*

Highlight range A2:F11 (whole table).

On **Borders** palette, click ▦ (inside vertical border).

  Vertical borders appear between columns of selection.

9 *Remove and restore borders*

Make sure range A2:F11 is still selected.

On **Borders** palette, click ▦ (no border).

  All borders in selection disappear.

On **Edit** menu, choose **Undo Borders** to restore borders.

10 *Close Borders palette*

11 *Save changed workbook file*

Complete previous activity before going on.

Add cell shading

You can also add a background color, a pattern, or a shade of gray to call attention to chosen cells.

1 **Add shading (method 1)**

In **Borders and Shading** pane of **Formatting Palette**, click 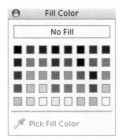 (fill color).

Click double-bar at top so menu becomes **Fill Color** palette.

Palette is torn off and remains in front of worksheet, ready for use.

Select cells in range B2:F2.

On **Fill Color** palette, click to select any light color or shade of gray.

Click anywhere on worksheet to deselect cells and see result.

Close palette.

2 **Add shading (method 2)**

Select range B8:E8.

On **Format** menu, choose **Cells**. Click **Patterns** in bar at top.

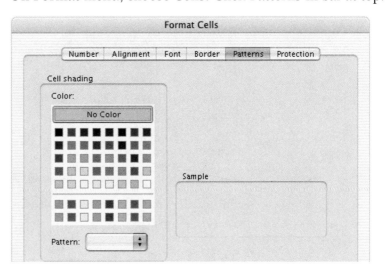

In **Color** area, click to select any light color or shade of gray.

Click ⬦ below color area to see **Pattern** pop-up menu.

Choose any light pattern with diagonal lines. Click **OK**.

Click anywhere on worksheet to deselect cells and see result.

3 **Save and close Plans workbook file**

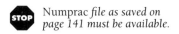

Format numbers

Numbers on a worksheet can be formatted to display dollar signs, commas, and fixed decimal points.

1 Open Numprac workbook file from your My Files folder

2 Apply number format (method 1)

Highlight cell range A3:D5.

In **Number** pane of **Formatting Palette**, view **Format** pop-up menu.

On menu, choose **Currency**.

3 Compare applied format with original data

Click anywhere to deselect block.

2				
3	$123.00	$321.00	$741.00	$1,471.00
4	$456.00	$654.00	$852.00	$2,582.00
5	$789.00	$987.00	$963.00	$3,693.00
6				

Formatted numbers have dollar signs, comma separators, and two decimal places.

Click any cell with number in new format. Look at formula bar.

Number remains as you entered it. Only format on worksheet has changed.

4 Apply percentage format

Select same range of cells.

Use same method to choose **Percentage** format.

2				
3	12300.00%	32100.00%	74100.00%	147100.00%
4	45600.00%	65400.00%	85200.00%	258200.00%
5	78900.00%	98700.00%	96300.00%	369300.00%
6				

Numbers have percent signs, no comma separators, and two decimal places.

5 Increase decimal places

If not highlighted, select data range A3:D5 again.

On **Formatting Palette**, click ⬆.0̥0̥ (increase decimal).

Numbers display three decimal places.

Click ⬆.0̥0̥ (increase decimal) again to add another decimal place.

Microsoft Excel adjusts column widths to accommodate longer numbers.

6 Decrease decimal places

On **Formatting Palette**, click .0̥0̥⬇ (decrease decimal) twice.

Numbers have two decimal places.

Click .0̥0̥⬇ (decrease decimal) twice more.

Numbers have no decimal places. Column widths remain widened.

7 **Apply accounting format**

Select same range of cells. Use same method to choose **Accounting** format.

2							
3	$	123.00	$	321.00	$	741.00	$	1,471.00
4	$	456.00	$	654.00	$	852.00	$	2,582.00
5	$	789.00	$	987.00	$	963.00	$	3,693.00
6							

Numbers have dollar signs lined up at left of cell, comma separators, and two decimal places. (Negative numbers would appear in parentheses.)

8 **Apply number format (method 2)**

If not highlighted, select data range A3:D5 again.

On **Format** menu, choose **Cells**. Click **Number** in bar at top.

In **Category** list, choose **Number**. Notice options available at right.

In addition to controlling decimal places and commas, you can choose four different ways to show negative numbers.

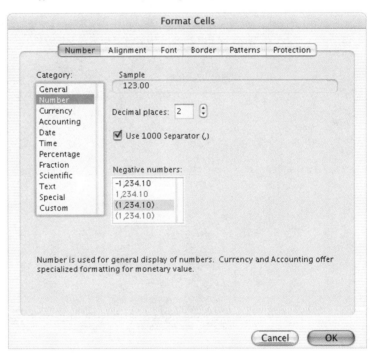

Click **OK**.

9 **Return numbers to General format**

Make sure that all cells with numbers are selected.

In **Number** pane of **Formatting Palette**, view **Format** pop-up menu. Choose **General**.

All special number formats are removed from selected cells.

10 **Close workbook file without saving changes**

Enter & format dates

Dates can be formatted in many styles. They're treated as numbers so that you can perform calculations with them.

1 *Open new workbook file*

Click 🗋 (new) on standard toolbar. Change view to normal.

2 *Enter date*

Click cell B2.

Enter today's date in month/day/year format (example: 9/1/05). Use two digits for year. Don't put leading zeros in month or day.

Click ✅. Check formula bar.

> *Excel recognized entry as date and changed year to four-digit number.*

Check worksheet cell.

> *Date appears on worksheet in format you used when entering data.*

By the way

The years 1930–2029 can safely be entered in two-digit form. If you need to enter other years, you must type all four digits.

3 *View current date format, and change it*

On **Format** menu, choose **Cells**. If necessary, click **Number** at top.

> *In Category list, Date is highlighted, showing that cell B2 contains date entry. Current format (3/14/01) is highlighted in Type list.*

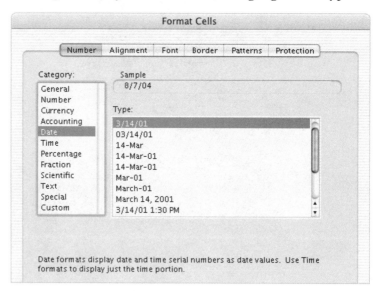

In **Type** list, click **14-Mar-01**. Click **OK**.

> *Format changes on worksheet, but entry (shown in formula bar) is same.*

By the way

In custom formats, m means the month number; mm means the month number with a leading zero for numbers less than 10; mmm means the three-letter month abbreviation; and mmmm means the full name of the month.

4 *Create new date format*

On **Format** menu, choose **Cells**. In **Category** list on **Number** page, click **Custom**.

Tap [TAB] until **Type** text box at top is highlighted.

Type mmmm d, yyyy and click **OK**.

> *Date appears with custom format. Column widens.*

Perform date calculation

Dates are really numbers formatted in a special way. You can do arithmetic with the numbers.

1 Enter another date

Click cell B3. Type date of your next birthday in m/d/yy format.

Click ✅ to accept entry.

Tip

You can also use the Format Painter *tool on the standard toolbar to copy formatting from one cell to another. Click the cell containing the format you want to copy, then click* Format Painter, *then click the cell where you want to apply the format.*

2 Apply new date format you created

With cell B3 selected, choose **Cells** on **Format** menu.

In **Category** list, click **Custom**. Scroll to bottom of **Type** list.

Your format (mmmm d, yyyy) is now listed.

Click your new format. Click **OK**.

3 Calculate how many days until your birthday

Click cell B5. Enter formula **=B3-B2** and click ✅.

Observe result.

Difference between any two dates equals number of days between them.

By the way

Times work almost the same way as dates. You can subtract one time from another and get the time difference. The difference is formatted as a time, however, not a number. You can read the difference directly in hours, minutes, and seconds.

4 Change date formats to numbers, and see what's happening

Highlight cells B2 and B3.

On **Format** menu, choose **Cells**. Look at **Category** list.

As expected, cells B2 and B3 have Date format. You'll now change it.

In **Category** list, choose **Number**.

Tap TAB until **Decimal places** is highlighted. Type **0** .

Click **OK**, and look at cells B2, B3, and B5.

All you changed was format. Dates really are numbers. That's why you can subtract one date from another, and get number.

By the way

If you're making changes in a worksheet, and suddenly your dates disappear and strange five-digit numbers show up, it usually means your dates have lost their formats. Just highlight the numbers, and reapply the date format you prefer. Your dates will reappear.

5 Find out what day 0 is

Click cell B7. Type number **0** (*not* letter O), and click ✅.

In **Number** pane of **Formatting Palette**, choose **Custom** on **Format** pop-up menu.

Shortcut takes you directly to Number *page of* Format Cells *dialog box with* Custom *selected on list at left.*

Scroll to bottom of **Type** list.

Click your new date format. Click **OK**.

Day 0 is January 1, 1904. Dates are measured from then.

6 Close workbook file without saving changes

On **File** menu, choose **Close**. Do not save changes.

Sort data

You can rearrange the order of rows of cells in a spreadsheet. You can use the sort tool on the toolbar or the menus.

1 **Open Plans workbook file from your My Files folder**

2 **Select cells to be sorted**

Highlight A2:D6. Notice that A2 is active cell.

If you did not do all previous activities, contents and formatting will vary.

	A	B	C	D	E	F	G	H
1				Computer Purchase Projections				
2		January	February	March	Totals by Computer	Percent of Total		
3	IBM	11	14	9	34	21%		
4	Dell	10	9	12	31	19%		
5	Apple	17	12	16	45	28%		
6	Sony	15	20	14	49	31%		

3 **Sort data (method 1)**

Tap TAB until **February** cell is active.

On standard toolbar, click 🔽 (sort ascending).

Highlighted rows are sorted based on column with active cell. All data for Dell are in row 3 because Dell's February number is smallest.

4 **Sort data (method 2)**

Make sure range A2:D6 is still selected.

On **Data** menu, choose **Sort**. View pop-up list at top.

Dialog box lets you choose column to sort on. You'll use column A.

On pop-up list, choose (**Column A**).

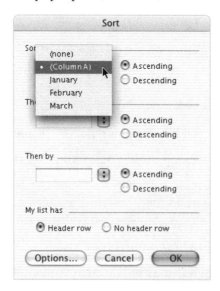

Notice near bottom that **Header row** option is already chosen.

To include top row of selection in sort, you would click No header row.

Click **OK**. Deselect highlighted block.

Apple is in top row.

5 *Use toolbar button to sort data so highest total is first*

Highlight A2:E6. Tap TAB until cell E2 (Totals by Computer) is active.

◇	A	B	C	D	E	F	G	H
1			**Computer Purchase Projections**					
2		January	February	March	Totals by Computer	Percent of Total		
3	*IBM*	11	14	9	34	21%		
4	*Dell*	10	9	12	31	19%		
5	*Apple*	17	12	16	45	28%		
6	*Sony*	15	20	14	49	31%		

On standard toolbar, click ▓ (sort descending).

> *Top seller (Sony) is now in top row.*

6 *Change sort to ascending by number*

On standard toolbar, click ▓ (sort ascending).

> *Computer with lowest total (Dell) is now in top row.*

7 *Sort table when selection includes column labels*

Highlight range A3:D6.

> *Row 2, with labels is no longer in selection. You want only data to be sorted.*

On **Data** menu, choose **Sort**.

Notice that **Header row** is selected near bottom of dialog box.

Click **No header row**.

Click **Descending** radio button at top.

Look at **Sort by** pop-up menu. On **Sort by** list, choose **Column D**.

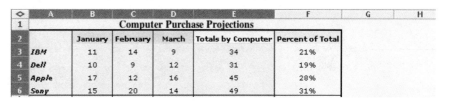

Tip

Think of the Then by areas of the Sort dialog box as "tie-breakers." If two rows of the selection have the same Sort by data, the rows are sorted according to the data in the Then by columns.

Click **OK**.

> *Rows in selection are now sorted in descending order of March projections.*

8 *Close workbook without saving changes*

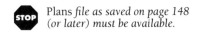

Plans *file as saved on page 148 (or later) must be available.*

Divide window into panes

When a worksheet is large, it's handy to divide the window into panes that keep important parts in view.

1   Open Plans workbook file from your My Files folder

— *Split bar before window is divided*

2   Split window into panes

Press and drag split bar (see figure at left) just below row 6.

Split bar being dragged —

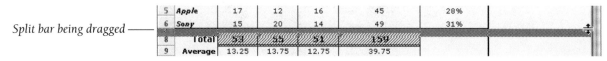

5	Apple	17	12	16	45	28%
6	Sony	15	20	14	49	31%
8	Total	53	55	51	159	
9	Average	13.25	13.75	12.75	39.75	

Two vertical scroll bars are now on right of window.

Use both scroll arrows in top pane to see whole worksheet.

Use both scroll arrows in bottom pane to see whole worksheet.

Each pane has separate view of same worksheet.

3   Lock labels in place in top pane

In top pane, scroll so rows 1 and 2 (table and column labels) are at top.

Press and drag split bar just under row 2 in top pane.

On **Window** menu, choose **Freeze Panes**.

Split is now single line. Only one vertical scroll bar appears.

Frozen rows in top pane —
Split line —
Scrolling rows in bottom pane —

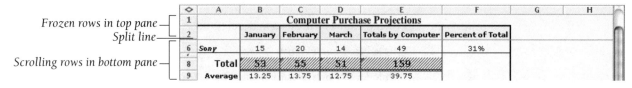

◇	A	B	C	D	E	F	G	H
1			Computer Purchase Projections					
2		January	February	March	Totals by Computer	Percent of Total		
6	Sony	15	20	14	49	31%		
8	Total	53	55	51	159			
9	Average	13.25	13.75	12.75	39.75			

Use scroll arrows to see what rows are available in lower pane.

Rows 1 and 2 are locked in top pane. Rest of worksheet scrolls in lower pane. Arrangement would be useful for table with many rows.

4   Unlock split, and remove split

On **Window** menu, choose **Unfreeze Panes**.

Split bar reappears.

On **Window** menu, choose **Remove Split** (or double-click split bar).

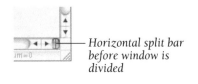

— *Horizontal split bar before window is divided*

5   Split window into left and right panes

Locate split bar at lower right, just right of horizontal scroll bar. Press and drag it just right of column A.

On **Window** menu, choose **Freeze Panes**. Scroll pane to right.

Labels stay in place at left.

Unfreeze panes. Remove split.

Tip

You can split a window or freeze panes vertically and horizontally at the same time. This is useful for locking labels both at the top and at the left of a large worksheet.

6   Close workbook without saving changes

STOP *Plans file as saved on page 148 (or later) must be available.*

Lock cells & protect worksheet

You can protect data in cells and their formats from accidental (or deliberate) changes.

STOP Plans *file as saved on page 148 (or later) must be available.*

Lock cells & protect worksheet

You can protect data in cells and their formats from accidental (or deliberate) changes.

1 *Open Plans workbook file from your My Files folder*

2 *Unlock cells where you want changes to be made*

Highlight data cells in range B3:D6.

> *These cells will be unlocked for possible changes in plan numbers.*

On **Format** menu, choose **Cells**; then click **Protection** in bar at top.

By the way

By default, all cells are locked. Locking has no effect, however, until protection of the worksheet is switched on (see step 3).

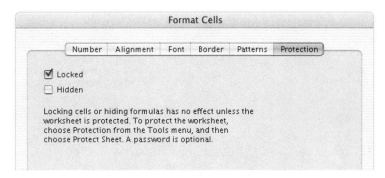

Click to remove mark from **Locked** check box; then click **OK**.

3 *Activate worksheet protection*

On **Tools** menu, choose **Protection**, then **Protect Sheet**.

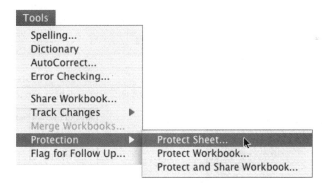

Protect Sheet *dialog box appears.*

By the way

The Protect Sheet *dialog box lets you enter a password so only you can turn protection off. You won't use this feature now.*

Click **OK**.

4 *Enter data in unlocked cell with protection turned on*

Click cell B5. Type 100 and tap RETURN.

> *New number is entered, and formulas recalculate.*

5 *Try to enter data in locked cell with protection turned on*

Click cell E5, and try to type 100.

> *Protected cells message appears.*

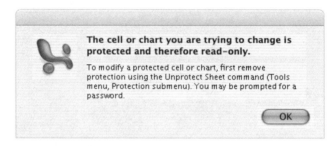

Click **OK**.

6 *Try to enter data in blank cell*

Click cell G3, and type 100. In protected cell message box, click **OK**.

By the way

Protection is used mainly by people who design spreadsheets for other people to use. The designer wants the user to simply enter certain data but not to change formulas, labels, or even formats.

7 *Try to change format of unlocked cell*

Click cell B5 (unlocked). Notice that **Formatting Palette** is not available (it is dimmed).

> *With protection on, you cannot change formatting of any cell on worksheet.*

8 *Remove protection*

On **Tools** menu, choose **Protection**, then **Unprotect Sheet**.

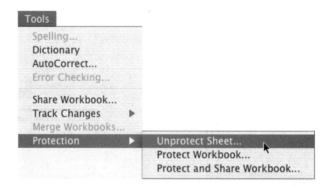

9 *Try to enter data in locked cell with protection turned off*

Click cell E5, type 100 and tap RETURN.

> *Number is entered, replacing formula there.*

10 *Close workbook without saving changes*

Create pie chart

After you create a worksheet table of numbers, you can quickly create a chart of the same data.

1 **Open Plans workbook file from your My Files folder**

2 **Select data to be charted**

Highlight range A2:A6 (names of brands).

With ⌘ held down, highlight range D2:D6 (totals for March).

Both ranges should be highlighted.

3 **Begin to create chart**

On **Insert** menu, choose **Chart** (or click 📊 on standard toolbar).

Step 1 of Chart Wizard *dialog box appears.*

4 **Choose chart type**

In **Chart type** list, click **Pie**.

In **Chart sub-type** area, accept default in upper left.

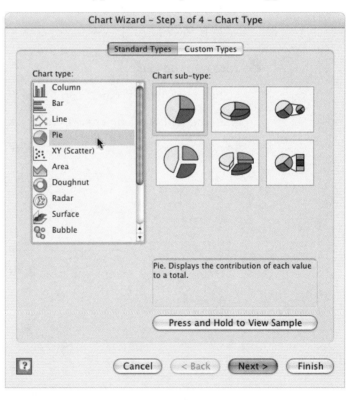

5 **Preview chart**

Position mouse pointer over **Press and Hold to View Sample** button.

Do what it says to see preview of chart.

Release mouse button.

6 **Click Next button to move to step 2**

Tip

When you click Next, *the* Back *button becomes active. You can always go back through steps and make changes.* Cancel *closes the* Chart Wizard *without making the chart.* Finish *ends the charting process using default settings.*

7   *Verify data to be charted*

Data range *shows two columns you highlighted in step 2.*

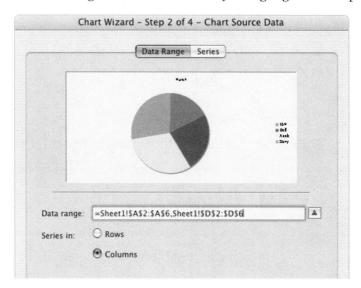

Click **Next** button to move to step 3.

8   *See chart options*

Click each part of bar at top to see options available.

You will make no changes here.

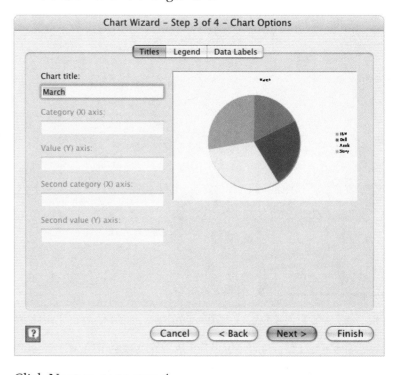

Click **Next** to go to step 4.

9 *Leave chart location in Sheet 1; click Finish button*

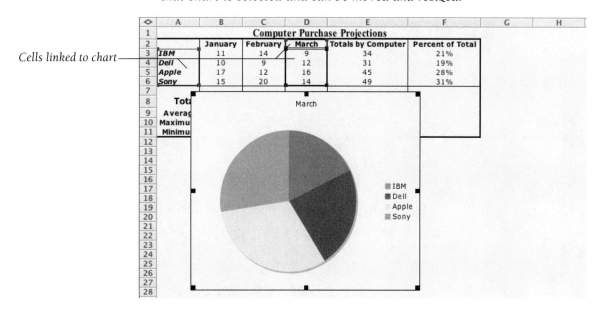

Chart appears on worksheet. Small black "handles" on edges of chart mean that chart is selected and can be moved and resized.

10 *Move chart if necessary*

Place pointer in clear area inside chart boundaries but outside pie. Press and drag chart down below all worksheet data.

11 *See link between chart and worksheet data*

Scroll up if necessary, and click cell D6 (March Sony projections).

Chart is no longer selected when you click cell.

Type 100 and tap RETURN. Notice changes in chart.

On standard toolbar, click ⟲ to undo editing change.

12 *Save changed workbook with new name*

On **File** menu, choose **Save As**. Type Charts as new file name.

Navigate to your **My Files** folder. Click **Save**.

Create column chart

You can put a chart on a separate sheet in the workbook. The chart is still linked to the data and will reflect changes.

1 Select data to chart

Highlight range A2:D6 (monthly projections with row and column labels).

2 Use Formatting Palette to create chart

At top of **Formatting Palette**, click **Add Objects** to see pane.

If necessary, click ▥ (charts) at top of pane.

> *Same chart types that you saw before appear here.*

Move pointer to figure of column chart. Click it.

> *Chart appears on same sheet as table.*

3 Move chart to sheet 2

With chart still selected, choose **Cut** on **Edit** menu.

At bottom of window, click **Sheet2** tab.

On **View** menu, choose **Normal**.

On **Edit** menu, choose **Paste**.

> *Chart is moved from sheet with data to blank sheet.*

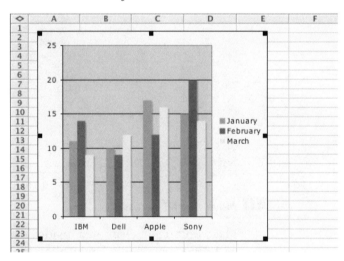

4 Switch between sheet with chart and worksheet

At bottom of window, click **Sheet1** tab to see worksheet.

Click **Sheet2** tab to return to sheet with chart.

5 Delete sheet 3, and rename others

Click **Sheet3** tab. On **Edit** menu, choose **Delete Sheet**. Click **OK**.

Click **Sheet1** tab; then double-click it. Type `Data` and tap (RETURN).

Click **Sheet2** tab. Click cell on worksheet to deselect chart.

Double-click **Sheet2** tab. Type `Chart` and tap (RETURN).

6 *Go to Data sheet and make changes*

Click **Data** tab.

Click cell D3 (March projections for IBM). Type 100 and tap RETURN.

Click **Chart** tab to see result in chart.

> *Chart is linked to cells in worksheet.*

Click 🔙 to undo change.

> *Undo takes you back to worksheet where you made change.*

Click **Chart** tab to see chart again.

7 *Use Formatting Palette to change chart type*

Click clear area of new chart. Look at **Formatting Palette**.

> *When chart is selected, palette has tools for modifying charts.*

Close **Add Objects** pane, and open **Chart Options** pane.

In **Chart Options** pane, click ▌▍ ▾ (chart type). On pop-up menu choose type shown in figure at left.

> *Chart type changes to 3-D effect. Data still come from same worksheet.*

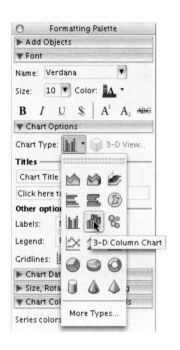

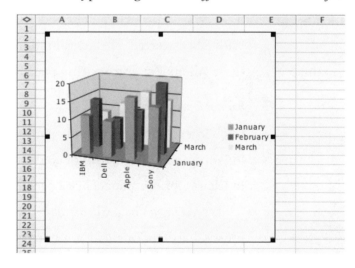

8 *Add title*

Click second item in **Titles** area of **Chart Options** pane.

Type First-Quarter Projections and tap RETURN.

> *Text appears as title on chart, and chart becomes smaller to make room.*

9 *Save changed Charts workbook file*

> *Sheet with data and sheet with chart are saved together in same file.*

Format chart text

You can format many objects on a chart. You'll use the Formatting Palette for this activity.

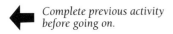

1 Format chart title

If chart title is not selected, click it.

> *When selected, chart title has thick border with small black selection handles.*

In **Font** pane of **Formatting Palette**, choose **16** on **Size** pop-up menu.

2 Add vertical-axis label, and format it

If necessary, open **Chart Options** pane on **Formatting Palette**.

> *If Chart Options is missing, it's because you accidentally clicked outside chart. Click chart to see panes for working with charts.*

Click pop-up menu below **Titles**. Choose **Z Axis Title**.

In text box below, type `Dozens to Purchase` and tap `RETURN`.

> *Text appears horizontally to left of vertical axis.*

Click new title to select it.

In **Font** pane, choose **12** on **Size** pop-up menu.

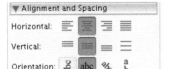

3 Change orientation of axis label

If necessary, open **Alignment and Spacing** pane on **Formatting Palette**.

With label selected, click **Orientation** button [abc] (rotate text up).

Close **Alignment and Spacing** pane on palette.

4 Format legend

Click legend (now to right of chart).

In **Font** pane of **Formatting Palette**, choose **12** on **Size** pop-up menu.

In **Chart Options** pane, click **Legend** pop-up menu. Choose **Bottom**.

> *Legend moves below chart and is arranged in single row.*

Close **Chart Options** pane on **Formatting Palette**.

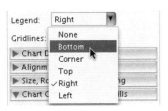

5 Format value axis labels

Click any number on vertical (value) axis. Notice handles at ends.

In **Font** pane, choose **12** on **Size** pop-up menu. Click [*I*].

> *Numbers on value axis become larger and are in italics.*

6 Save changed Charts workbook file

Complete previous activity before going on.

Format chart objects

After creating a chart, you can change the colors used, dimensions, axis scale, number formats, and other attributes.

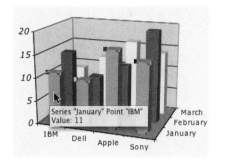

1 Format data series

Make sure that **Charts** workbook is open and **Chart** sheet is in view.

Click any blue column on chart. Notice handles on other blue columns.

> *Blue columns are for January "data series."*

Double-click any blue column to see formatting dialog box.

If necessary, click **Colors and Lines** in bar at top.

Format Data Series

| Colors and Lines | Shape | Labels | Order | Options |

Fill

Color: [ ] ☐ Invert if negative

Transparency: 0 ○——— 100 0 % ⬍

Line

Color: No Line ⬍ Style: ·············· ⬍

Dashed: ——— ⬍ Weight: 0 ⬍ pts

Transparency: 0 ○——— 100 0 % ⬍

In **Fill** area, choose new color for faces of columns.

Change **Transparency** to **30%** so that rear columns are more visible.

In **Line** area, make any changes you like to edges of columns.

Explore **Shape** and other pages of dialog box, but don't make changes there.

Click **OK**. Look at changes you made to front columns.

> *You can undo formatting change if you don't like it.*

2 Explore other features you can change

Move pointer to each part of chart, and see what text appears below pointer.

> *Text identifies separate parts of chart. Double-clicking opens dialog box for formatting and changing part.*

3 Format chart area

Put pointer on clear area near border around chart. When **Chart Area** tip box appears at pointer, double-click.

Use **Format Chart Area** dialog box to change fill color to light yellow.

Explore other pages of dialog box.

Click **OK** to see change.

4 *Remove line on vertical (value) axis*

Put pointer on any number on vertical axis. When **Value Axis** tip box appears, double-click.

Click **Colors and Lines** in bar at top if necessary.

Use **Color** pop-up menu to choose **No Line**.

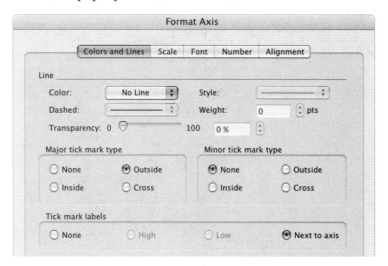

5 *Change scale on axis*

Click **Scale** in bar at top. Change number in **Major unit** text box to **2**.

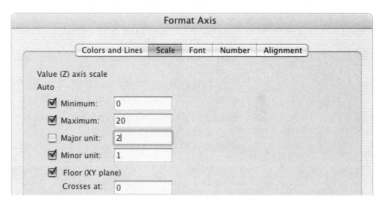

6 *View chart with modifications*

Click **OK**. Notice both changes on vertical axis.

7 *Make additional changes to chart if you wish*

8 *Save changed Charts workbook*

9 *Quit Microsoft Excel, and shut down computer*

On **Excel** menu, choose **Quit Excel**.

If you're using floppy disk, eject it as shown on page 5, step 5.

On Apple menu, choose **Shut Down**.

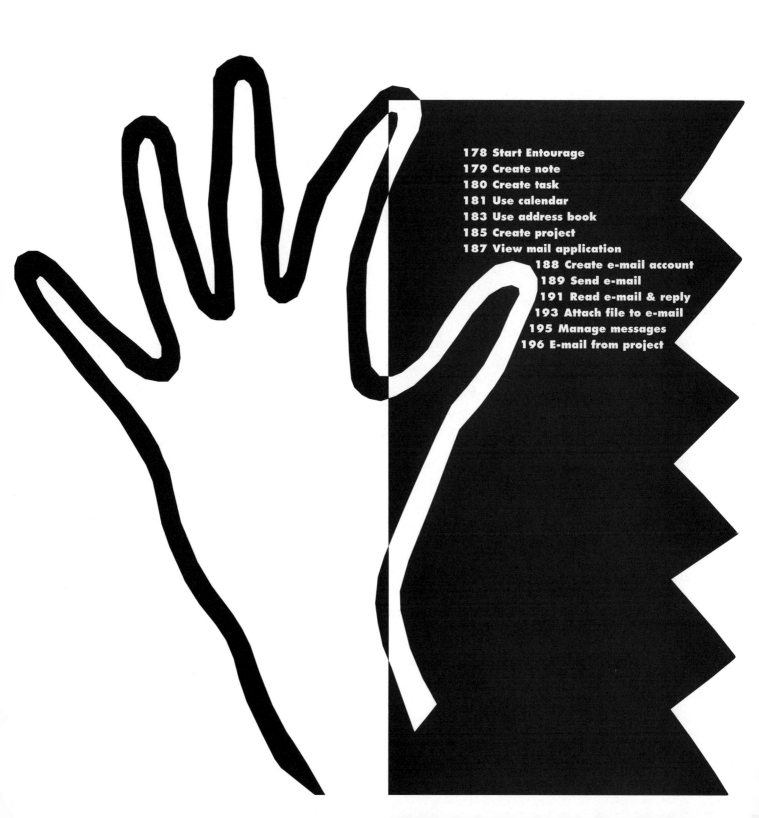

Start Entourage

Microsoft Entourage consists of six applications that work together. You'll now prepare Entourage for future activities.

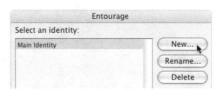

By the way

If several people use the same log-in account on the Macintosh, Entourage identities allow them to keep their e-mail, calendar, projects, and so forth, separate from one another.

Tip

Whenever you start Entourage in the future, make sure your name is in the title bar. If not, choose Switch Identity *on the* Entourage *menu, and double-click your name.*

IMPORTANT

If you quit Entourage, end a session at the computer, and later return, you must be sure to log in to the same user account you're using now. All settings you make and items you save will be stored in a folder belonging to that user account. (This means that floppy disk and thumb drive users will not be able to take their Entourage work to another computer.)

1 Start Microsoft Entourage

Start computer. Start program as on page 7, but choose **Microsoft Entourage** or its icon.

> Entourage *menu bar appears with large document window below.*

Close any dialog box or window that appears in front of main window.

2 Create new identity

On **Entourage** menu, choose **Switch Identity**. Click **Switch** to approve.

At right of **Entourage** dialog box, click **New**.

In **New Identity** dialog box, type your name. Click **OK**.

Cancel dialog box that appears. Close **Entourage Setup Assistant** window.

> *Title bar of main Entourage window includes your name.* Mail *is one part of Entourage. As you use other parts, their names will replace* Mail.

3 Make preference changes expected in this book

On **View** menu, make sure **Toolbars** and **Folders List** are checked and **Preview Pane** is set to **On Right**.

On **Entourage** menu, choose **Preferences**.

In left pane, click **Address Book**. Enter your area code in text box.

In left pane, click **Spelling**. Remove check from **Check spelling as you type**. Click **OK** to accept changes.

4 Disable AutoCorrect feature

On **Tools** menu, choose **AutoCorrect**.

On **AutoCorrect** page, deselect all options. On **AutoFormat** page, deselect first two options. Click **OK** to accept all changes.

5 Zoom window out

At left of title bar, click (zoom) to enlarge window.

> *You may also drag borders between panes to change relative sizes.*

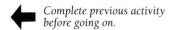
Complete previous activity before going on.

Create note

The Notes application is the simplest in Entourage. You use it to create and organize notes you want to remember.

1 Switch to Notes

Look at six buttons at top of left pane of window.

> *Buttons let you move to different applications. Highlight shows current one.*

In left pane, click **Notes**.

Notice items (mostly dimmed now) on toolbar for working with notes.

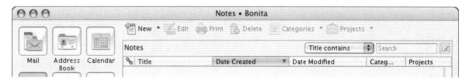

2 Create new note

On toolbar, click 📝 New to open window for creating note.

Enter text in figure below. Tap TAB to move from **Title** to body of note.

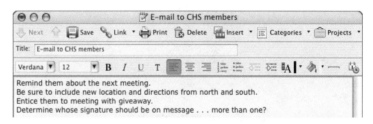

3 Save note, and close note window

Click 💾 Save on toolbar. Click 🔴🟡🟢 (close).

> *Title of note appears in Notes window.*

Click note to select it. Notice that toolbar items are no longer dimmed.

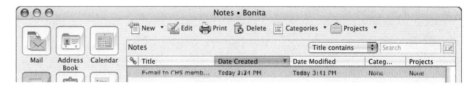

By the way

Don't look for saved notes in your My Files folder. They're saved in a folder that was created when you set up a new identity in step 2 on page 178. (See also the Important box in the margin on that page.)

4 Create category, and apply to note

On toolbar, click arrow at right of 📋 Categories ▾. On pop-up menu, choose **Edit Categories**.

In new window, click ➕ Add Category .

Type `Comp Hist` as name. Choose color at right. Close window.

> *New category is created. Now you can apply it.*

With note selected, click arrow at right of 📋 Categories ▾. On pop-up menu, choose **Comp Hist**.

> *You'll use note when you learn about projects on page 185.*

By the way

A category you create in one part of Entourage is available in all other parts. You'll use this one again.

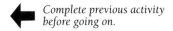
Create task

A task is a "to do" item to remind you that you need to take care of something. It's like a note but has a due date attached.

Tip

To get more room in the right pane, you can hide the left pane in all main Entourage windows. Click ◂▥ (hide views) in the left pane. The six application buttons become smaller versions at the far left. The button changes to ▥▸ (show views).

1   **Switch to Tasks**

In left pane of main window, click **Tasks** button.

2   **Create new task**

On toolbar, click ☑ New .

In **Task** text box, type `Send e-mail to members`.

Click check boxes, and enter **Due date** and **Reminder** date and time.

> *You can click small calendar icon at right of* Due date *and* Reminder *text boxes to choose date from calendar.*

Select **High** from **Priority** pop-up list.

3   **Assign category to task**

On toolbar, click arrow at right of ▤ Categories ▾ .

On pop-up menu, choose **Comp Hist** category you created on page 179.

4   **Save task, and close window**

Click 💾 Save on toolbar. Click ⊗ ⊖ ⊕ to close window.

> *Task header appears in Tasks window.*

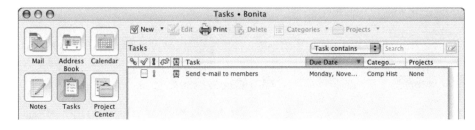

5   **Reopen task for possible editing**

Click anywhere in task header.

> *You can use buttons on toolbar to edit, print, or delete task.*

On toolbar, click ☑ Edit to open task for changes. You won't make any.

Close window.

An Entourage window must be open.

Use calendar

The Calendar application lets you put events on a calendar you can view by day, week, or month.

Tip

If the main window is ever closed, there's another way to navigate in Entourage. On the View menu, choose Go To, then the name of the Entourage application you want. (The View menu name changes to Calendar when the latter application is running.)

Tip

In Calendar, as in all Microsoft Office applications, you can drag pane borders to make some panes bigger, others smaller.

1   Switch to Calendar

In group of application buttons at the left, click **Calendar**. If necessary, click ▦ Month on toolbar.

Current month appears with today's date highlighted.

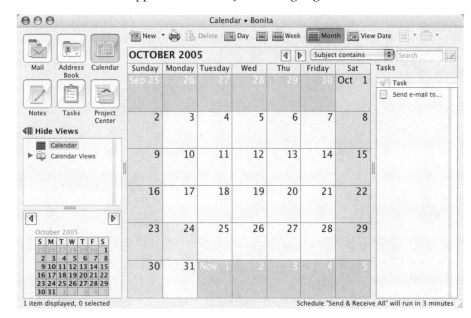

2   See other dates

At top of center pane, click either button (◀ ▶) to change month.

On toolbar, click ▦ View Date . Type 12/2007 and click **OK**.

To return to today, on **Calendar** menu choose **Go to Today** (or tap ⌘ T).

3   See other views

On toolbar, click ▦ Week . Notice that rows are now hours of day.

Miniature calendar at left highlights week that appears in center pane.

Click different week on miniature to change week.

Explore **Work Week** and **Day** views. On miniature, click different days.

Tap ⌘ T to return to today. Click ▦ Month to change back to **Month** view.

4   Create calendar event

Double-click square of any day on calendar.

New untitled window opens, where you can enter information about event.

In **Subject** text box, type My birthday and tap TAB.

Use calendar *continued*

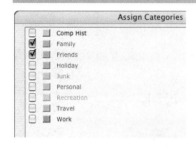

5 *Choose category*

Click [≣ Categories] (*not* arrow). Click **Family** and **Friends** check boxes. Click **OK**.

You can create special views to see events in only certain categories.

6 *Change date, and add reminder*

Notice **Start** and **End** dates are same as date you double-clicked.

If event were that day, you'd be set. It probably isn't, so you'll change date.

Click [▦] to right of start date. On miniature calendar, click arrow buttons to navigate to month of your next birthday. Then click date.

If necessary, put check in **Reminder** check box, then click [minutes ▾] to see options for giving advance notice of event.

7 *Make it recurring event, and add comment*

On **Occurs** pop-up menu, choose **Every** followed by event date.

Click in large text area at bottom of **My Birthday** event window.

Type Another one!

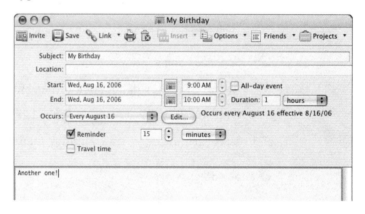

On toolbar of event window, click [💾 Save]. Then close window.

8 *Find and edit event*

On calendar toolbar, click [▦ View Date]. Type next birthday, and click **OK**.

Put pointer on event to see full text, if necessary.

Double-click event. Click **Open this one**. Click **OK** to see event window.

Changes you make here affect this event, not all occurrences.

Enter start time for planned birthday party.

On toolbar of event window, click [💾 Save]. Then close window.

Tap [⌘ T] to return to today's date.

An *Entourage window must be open.*

Use address book

The Address Book application lets you store and organize information about family, friends, and business contacts.

1 Switch to Address Book

In left pane, click **Address Book**. Look at top pane at right.

Header is for whoever installed Microsoft Office.

Above header line, look at types of information you can enter for person.

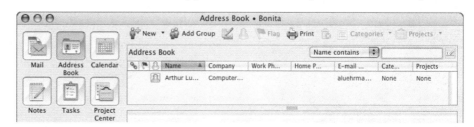

2 Add new contacts

On toolbar, click **New**. Enter data in figure at left.

When finished, click **Save & New** at top to save contact and clear window.

Add another contact, using same **Company** name (make up e-mail address and other data).

Add yourself (if not already listed). Include your actual e-mail address.

Add another contact. When finished, click **Save & Close**.

New headers appear in top pane. You can drag pane border down to see all.

3 Edit contact information

Double-click **Kendall Hunt** header.

Window opens with person's name in title bar.

Click each item in bar at top to see separate pages with information.

On **Name & E-mail** page, click inside large **E-mail** box. Click **Add** to right of **E-mail** box.

To left of new text box, click **Home**. On pop-up menu choose **Other e-mail**.

In new text box, type `kgh127@aol.com` as address.

Click **Make Default** to make this main address for e-mail.

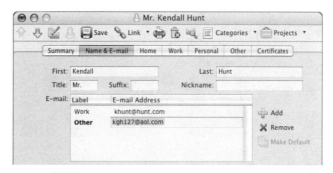

Click **Save** to save changes. Close **Mr. Kendall Hunt** window.

IMPORTANT

If you'll be doing the activities beginning on page 188, your own contact must have your actual e-mail address. If necessary, double-click your contact header, and add or change the e-mail address.

Tip

Typing an e-mail address correctly is tricky. Do it once in the address book. Then, when you're ready to send e-mail, it takes only a few clicks to add the correct address.

4　Sort address book by data field

In top pane, notice field names (column headings) above contact headers.

Highlighted Name *field means headers are now sorted by last name.*

By the way
You can reverse the sort order by clicking the sort field again.

Click **Company** to sort list on this data field.

Sorting on company name groups people from same company and could help you find employee whose name you'd forgotten.

5　Search for contacts

Click [Name contains ⬍] to see pop-up menu. Chose **Company contains**.

Type `hun` and notice that only matching headers appear now.

To right of search box, click ✏ (clear) to bring back all contacts.

6　Categorize contacts

If necessary, sort headers by company name. Click first header with **Hunt** as start of company name. With (SHIFT) held down, click second one.

On toolbar, click arrow at right of ▤ Categories ▾ to see pop-up menu.

On menu, choose **Comp Hist** category you created on page 179.

Category is applied to contacts you selected. After applying categories, you can sort and search by category.

7　Create contact group

Make sure same contacts are still selected.

By the way
You can add the same person to more than one group. A group is just a set of pointers to contacts, which remain in the address book as separate entries.

On toolbar, click 👥 Add Group . Type `CHS` as name of group.

Window allows you to add or remove contacts. Selected contacts are already in window. You could add others by clicking ➕ in toolbar.

On **CHS** toolbar, click 💾 (save group). Close **CHS** window.

In top pane of **Address Book** window, notice 👥 (group icon) to left of **CHS**.

New contact group ——

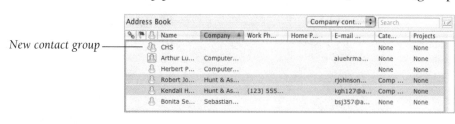

← *Complete all previous Entourage activities before going on.*

Create project

A project is a central place where you can put a group of related notes, tasks, contacts, e-mail, and even documents.

1 **Switch to Project Center**

In group of application buttons at left, click **Project Center**.

2 **Create new project**

On toolbar, click [New Project] . Enter data shown below, with due date in future.

By the way

Page 2 of the New Project Wizard lets you automatically add existing items to the project. You'll skip that feature now, so you can learn how to make manual additions.

Click ▶ at bottom of dialog box to go to page 2. Make no changes.

Click ▶ to go to page 3. Remove mark from bottom check box.

Continue to page 4, and click ▶ to finish.

Overview of new project appears in Project Center *window.*

Near middle of window, click **New & Recent Mail**. On pop-up menu, choose **Recent Items**.

Changes you make to project will show up under this heading.

New project ——

Project overview ——

3 **Add existing note to project**

At lower right, click ⊕ (add); on pop-up menu, choose **Note**.

Add Note window lists all notes you've created.

Click name of note you created on page 179. Click **Add**.

Notice name of note now under **Recent Items**. Click it to see contents. Then close note window.

By the way

Removing an item from a project does not delete it. If you switched to the Notes application now, you would see your note listed there.

4 **Remove note from project**

In bar at top below toolbar, click **Notes**.

> Project Center *window now shows all notes belonging to project.*

Click note you just added. At bottom of window, click ⊗ (remove).

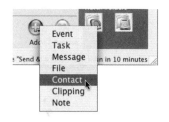

5 **Add contacts to project**

In bar at top below toolbar, click **Overview**.

At lower right, click ⊕ ; on pop-up menu, choose **Contact**.

In **Add Contact** window, sort existing contacts on **Categories**.

Select both contacts with category **Comp Hist**. Click **Add**.

6 **Add new task to project**

On toolbar, click arrow at right of 🖉 New ▾; from pop-up menu, choose **Task**.

Enter details for task like those shown below.

Click 🖫 Save , and close window. Notice task header now in overview window.

7 **Add file to project**

If you're using floppy disk for saved files, make sure it's in drive.

At lower right, click ⊕ ; on pop-up menu, choose **File**.

> Add File *dialog box works exactly same way as* Open.

Navigate to your **My Files** folder (see page 21, step 2).

In right pane, locate **Slides.ppt** (or another file). Double-click it.

By the way

The file itself remains where it was. What gets added to the project is a pointer to the location of the file.

8 **Open file from project window**

In row of buttons below toolbar, click **Files**. Double-click file just added.

After file opens, quit **PowerPoint** (or other application) when ready.

An Entourage window
must be open.

View mail application

You don't have to be connected to the Internet to learn the main
features of the Mail application in Entourage.

1 Switch to Mail

In group of application buttons at left, click **Mail**.

2 View mailboxes

In left pane, look at list of mail boxes. Notice one labeled **Inbox (1)**.

Number in parentheses tells how many unread e-mails you have.

3 Read e-mail

In middle pane, notice header beginning **The Microsoft Mac....**

Header shows e-mail sender and subject (cut off to fit in pane).

4 Click anywhere in header to see contents of message in right pane.

Message contains attached files. You'll learn about them on page 193.

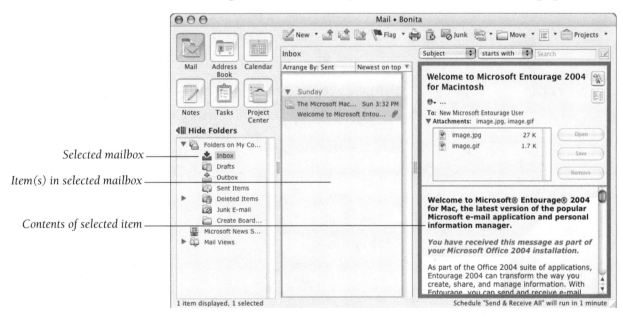

Selected mailbox

Item(s) in selected mailbox

Contents of selected item

5 Open e-mail in separate window

In middle pane, double-click header.

Close new window when finished reading message.

6 Delete e-mail

Put pointer on each tool in toolbar to see what you can do with e-mail.

With header selected in middle pane, click 🗑 (delete) on toolbar.

In left pane, click **Deleted Items**. Notice header in middle pane.

7 Quit Entourage

*There's no prompt about saving your work. All changes you've made since
starting Entourage were automatically saved when you made them.*

By the way

E-mail remains in the Deleted
Items *mailbox until you empty it.
To do so, hold down* CONTROL *as
you click the mailbox, and choose*
Empty 'Deleted Items' *on the pop-
up menu.*

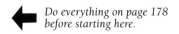 *Do everything on page 178 before starting here.*

Create e-mail account

For the rest of the activities in this book, you need to set up an e-mail account in Entourage and use it to connect to the Internet.

By the way

If you'll be using a modem to dial up a connection to your ISP, you must first set up the modem properly and provide the telephone number, your log-in name, and your password. Use the Network system preference.

Tip

If you already have an e-mail account set up in an older version of Entourage on this computer or in another e-mail program, such as Mail, you can use the Import command on the File menu to set up your new account here.

---

1 Use Mail application

Start Entourage (see page 178).

If your name isn't on title bar, choose **Switch Identities** on **Entourage** menu. Click **Switch** to approve. Then choose your **name** on list.

If necessary, click **Mail** at upper left of window to switch to e-mail application.

2 Begin account setup

On **Tools** menu, choose **Accounts**. On **Mail** page, click ✳ New .

> Account Setup Assistant *dialog box appears.*

3 Try for quick setup

Make sure your computer is connected to the Internet.

Type existing e-mail address in text box. If computer is connected to Microsoft Exchange Server, click check box at bottom.

Click ▶ to move to next page of assistant.

If page 2 of assistant says **Automatic Configuration Failed**, skip to step 4.

Otherwise, go to page 3 of assistant, enter password, and skip to step 5.

4 Set up account manually

Click ▶ to move to page 3 of assistant. Enter information provided to you by your Internet Service Provider (ISP).

Information	*Typical example*
your name	John Smith
e-mail address	jsmith@yourisp.com
account ID	jsmith
your e-mail password	2secret3 (*substitute yours*)
incoming mail server name	mail.yourisp.com
type of incoming mail server	POP or IMAP
outgoing mail server name	smtp.yourisp.com

5 Verify account settings, and finish setup

Click ▶ to move to next page of assistant. Click **Verify My Settings**.

> *Computer tries to log into account. If not successful, you must go back and make changes.*

Go to last page of assistant. Enter name for account (your ISP, for example), and click **Finish**.

> *Name you gave appears in* Accounts *window.*

Close **Accounts** window.

Send e-mail

You'll use the Entourage Mail application to send an e-mail message over the Internet.

1 Start message

With any mailbox selected at left, click ![New] (new message) on toolbar.

Two windows appear in front of Mail *window. Front window is where you enter e-mail address of person you're sending message to.*

On toolbar of front window, click 🔲 to see address book items at right.

2 Enter address (method 1)

Click anywhere in big **To** box. Begin typing your own name or address.

Full name and address appear below typing. They came from address book.

By the way

You'll be sending to your own e-mail address so you'll have a message to open and read on page 191. Make sure your e-mail address here is the same as the one you entered when setting up the account on page 188.

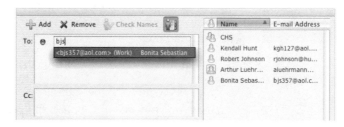

Tap [TAB] to accept suggested text (or keep typing if it's not what you want).

3 Enter address (method 2)

In address book pane, double-click row for **Kendall Hunt**.

4 Change address of person with two e-mail addresses

With [CONTROL] held down, click **Kendall Hunt** in To box at left.

On pop-up menu, choose address *not* labeled (**Default**).

5 Delete address

Make sure **Kendall Hunt** is selected in list at left. On toolbar, click [✖ Remove].

6 Type subject and message

You could also use Cc box to send copies. Instead, you'll finish message.

Tap [RETURN] to complete entry and close front window.

In **Subject** box, type brief topic. Tap [TAB]. Look at title bar.

In message area below, type your message.

Message window should look similar to figure below.

Tip

Think of your subject text as a headline that will make the purpose of your e-mail clear to the reader.

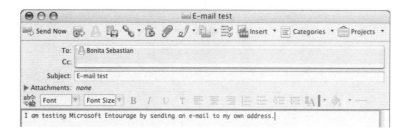

7 *Make Progress window visible*

On **Window** menu, choose **Progress**. Drag window below message window.

You may have to raise bottom of message window to make room.

8 *View sending options*

Click message window to activate it.

On toolbar, locate  (send later), and (save as draft).

Sending later is useful when you have several messages to send, and you want to send all at once. Saving as draft is for unfinished messages.

9 *Send message now*

On toolbar, click . Watch **Progress** window.

Progress window shows activity. Connections to Internet vary. You may be asked for your account name and password.

After connection is complete, e-mail is sent, and message window closes.

Close **Progress** window.

10 *See items sent*

In left pane of **Mail** window, click **Sent Items**.

Header for item you sent is listed in middle pane.

Click header in center pane to see message in right pane.

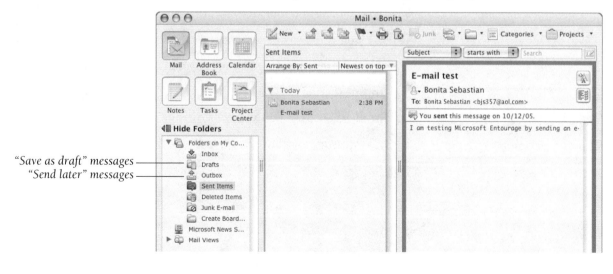

← *Complete previous activity before going on.*

Read e-mail & reply

Entourage allows you to receive and view any e-mail that has been sent to you.

By the way

If you have more than one e-mail account, you can receive mail from one at a time. Click the down-arrow to the right of the Send & Receive button. Choose the account you want to get mail from.

1 Get e-mail

On toolbar of **Mail** window, click 📧 (send & receive).

> *Button sends any Outbox messages, then gets messages sent to you.*

Wait for **Inbox** to become bold and show one (or more) unread messages.

> *You may have to repeat first step, depending on network activity.*

2 View contents of inbox

Click **Inbox** in left pane to see message headers in center pane.

In center pane, notice header(s) for message(s) received.

> *Bold type in header means you haven't read message yet.*

3 Read message

In center pane, click item you just got. Read message in right pane.

By the way

When you click or double-click an item in the inbox, the message remains in the inbox but is marked as having been read by you. (The boldface disappears from the item header.)

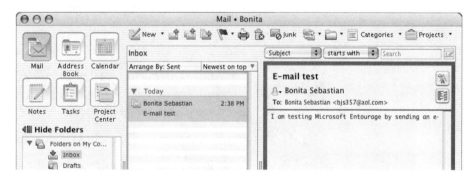

Double-click same header to open message in separate window.

> *Pane at top shows sender, date, recipient, and subject. Message is below.*

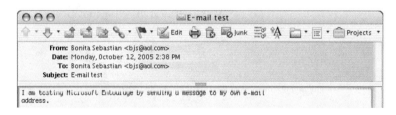

Tip

Click Reply All if you want to send a reply to the sender and everyone else the message was sent to.

4 Create reply to message

On toolbar of message window, click 📤 (reply).

> *New message window appears, in which you can type your reply. To and Subject are automatically filled out. (You can edit them, though.)*

Look at bottom pane of message window.

> *Message you're replying to normally appears there in blue type with each line preceded by angle bracket (>).*

Tip

It's good practice when replying to e-mail to include all or at least the important parts of the message you're replying to.

Type your reply.

> *Message window should look similar to figure on next page.*

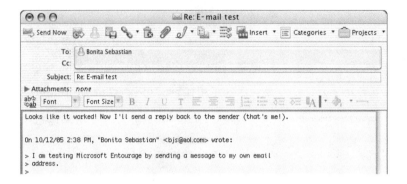

5 Send reply

On toolbar of message window, click .

After reply is sent, close original message window.

At right of **Mail** window, notice yellow bar saying you've replied.

In header in center pane, notice symbol at lower right.

Curved arrow means you've replied to message.

6 Read reply just sent (to yourself)

On Entourage toolbar, click 🗩 (send & receive).

Wait for new item to appear in **Inbox**.

With **Inbox** highlighted at left, click new header in center pane.

Notice contents of message in right pane.

Message is reply you just sent to yourself.

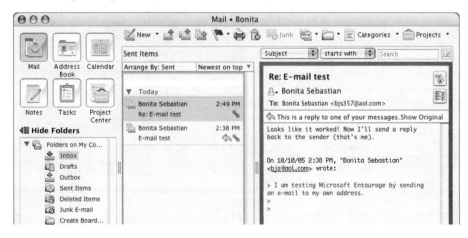

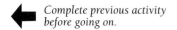*Complete previous activity before going on.*

Attach file to e-mail

You can attach Microsoft Word documents, pictures, music, or any other type of file when you send e-mail.

1 Create new message

On toolbar, click 🖉 New . Address message to yourself. Tap (RETURN).

In **Subject** text box, type File attachment test.

2 Attach file to message

If using floppy disk, insert it in drive now.

On Mail toolbar, click 📎 (add attachments).

> *File navigation dialog box appears. It works exactly like* Open *dialog box.*

Navigate to your **My Files** folder (see page 21, step 2).

Scroll list of files you've created, and double-click one you will attach.

> *Name of file appears after* Attachments *label, just below* Subject.

If necessary, click triangle to left of **Attachments** to see box below it.

3 Add message, and send

Type message similar to one at bottom of figure below.

Attached files listed here ——

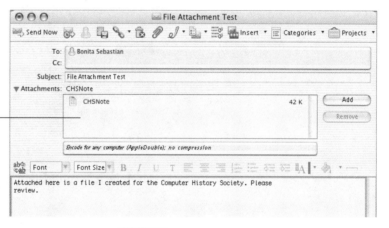

On toolbar, click 📨 Send Now button. Wait for message to be sent.

4 Get message

Click 📧 (send & receive). Wait for message to be received.

With **Inbox** highlighted, notice paper-clip icon at bottom right of new header.

> *Paper clip means message has file attached.*

In center pane, click new header. Look at right pane.

> *Window should look similar to top figure on next page.*

5 *Save copy of attached file*

In **Attachments** scroll box, click name of attached file.

At right, click **Save** button, as in figure below.

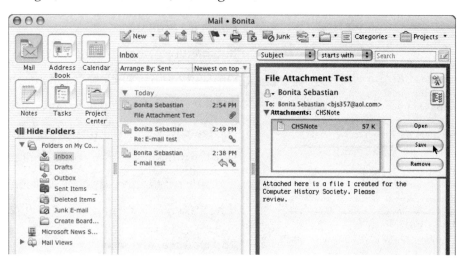

6 *Pay attention to warning advice that appears*

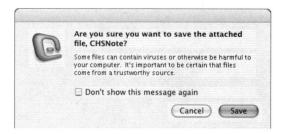

7 *Assuming you trust yourself, complete operation*

Click **Save**.

> Save Attachment *dialog box appears. It works same way as Save dialog box.*

In **Save As** text box, type `Received File`.

Navigate to your **My Files** folder (see page 19, step 2).

Click **Save**.

> *Copy of attached file is saved in your My Files folder.*

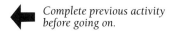

Complete previous activity before going on.

Manage messages

In just a few weeks of e-mail use, your Inbox *and* Sent Items *folders can become packed. Entourage can help.*

1 **Delete messages you no longer want**

In left pane, click **Sent Items**. In center pane, notice headers for sent e-mail.

Click first header. On toolbar, click 🗑 (delete). Repeat for second header.

Tip

You can also delete a message by dragging the header into the Deleted Items *folder.*

---

2 **View deleted items, and restore one**

In left pane, click **Deleted Items**. In center pane, notice headers.

> *Deleted items are still available. Here's how to get one back.*

Press and drag first header from center pane to **Sent Items** in left pane.

Click **Sent Items** to see item restored. Then delete it again.

3 **Permanently erase deleted items**

Hold down (CONTROL). In left pane, click **Deleted Items** folder.

On pop-up menu, choose **Empty 'Deleted Items'**.

> *Message warns that items will be permanently erased.*

Click **Empty** to approve erasure.

4 **Manage inbox items**

In left pane, click **Inbox**. On **View** menu, choose **Unread Only**.

> *Command is useful when inbox has lots of old e-mail you don't want to see.*

Choose same command (now checked) to see all headers again.

Click first header in list. On toolbar, click 🚩 (flag).

> *Flagging reminds you that you need to deal with item later.*

On **View** menu, choose **Flagged Only** to see unfinished business.

With message still selected, choose same command (now checked). On toolbar, click 🚩 again to remove flag.

5 **Create new folder for storing messages you've read**

If necessary, click **Inbox** in left pane. On **File** menu, choose **New**, then **Subfolder**.

Type Seen and tap (RETURN). Click **Inbox**. Click first header at right.

With (SHIFT) held down, click last header of messages you've read.

Press and drag selection to **Seen** subfolder. Click **Seen** subfolder.

> *Selected items disappear from* Inbox *but are still available.*

6 **Move items back to Inbox; delete new folder**

Select and drag items to **Inbox** to put them back where they were.

With **Seen** selected at left, click 🗑. Empty **Deleted Items** (see step 3).

Complete activity beginning on page 185 before going on.

E-mail from project

You can use most mail features from the Project Center. That makes it easy to manage messages to and from project people.

1 View existing project

In left pane of main window, click **Project Center** button.

In right pane, double-click **Create Board of Directors** header.

> *Overview page of project you created on page 185 appears.*

Look at **Recent Items** list in middle of page.

> *List shows task, two contacts, and one file you added to project earlier.*

2 View project contacts

Click **Contacts** in bar near top of window. Notice contacts you added.

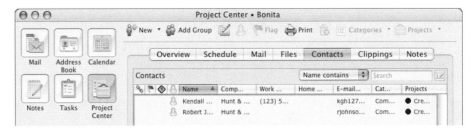

3 Prepare to send e-mail to project contacts

Click first contact in list. With (SHIFT) held down, click second one.

On **Contact** menu, choose **New Message To**.

> *Usual message window appears, with selected contacts in* **To** *box.*

> *Next step would be to finish message, and click* 📧 Send Now *. You won't do this now, because e-mail addresses you entered for contacts are fictitious.*

4 Cancel message, and look at Mail page of Project Center

Close message window.

Click **Mail** in bar near top of window.

> *Mail page of Project Center will show mail to and from project contacts only. No other distracting messages will appear here.*

5 End Microsoft Office 2004 activities

On **Entourage** menu, choose **Quit Entourage**.

If you're using floppy disk, eject it as shown on page 5, step 5.

On Apple menu, choose **Shut Down**.